T0147761

Voices of Our Veterans

Honoring the War Veterans of Mason County, West Virginia

Mr. Walter Raynes's Eleventh Grade Language Arts Students, 2009

iUniverse, Inc.
New York   Bloomington

Voices of Our Veterans
Honoring the War Veterans of Mason County, West Virginia

iUniverse books may be ordered through booksellers or by contacting:

iUniverse
1663 Liberty Drive
Bloomington, IN 47403
www.iuniverse.com
1-800-Authors (1-800-288-4677)

Because of the dynamic nature of the Internet, any Web addresses or links contained in this book may have changed since publication and may no longer be valid.

ISBN: 978-1-4401-9330-9 (sc)
ISBN: 978-1-4401-9328-6 (dj)
ISBN: 978-1-4401-9329-3 (ebk)

Printed in the United States of America

iUniverse rev. date: 1/13/2010

*To all American veterans who sacrificed so much for
the preservation of our freedom.*

The Authors. First Row (L-R): Tory Raynes, Deidra Peters, Hannah Foreman, Randi Roush, Taylor Hysell, Kaula Young, and Lindsey Deem. Second Row (Seated L-R): Kierstan White, Miriam Gordon. Third Row: Nathan Stewart, Robert Zerkle, Zach Whitlatch, Micaiah Branch. Fourth Row: Michael Fisher, Ethan McGrew, Brandon Johnson, Terry Henry, Scott Scarberry. Fifth Row: Sam German, Tim Roush. Not pictured: Colin Pierce, Zach Jividen, Kylee Henry, Tiffanie Miller.

Table of Contents

Foreword

The stories and experiences shared in this book are from veterans who are walking libraries that only war and military service can provide. The freedoms we enjoy every day are the result of their sacrifices, and generations of young men and women who in the past and in the present heroically and courageously answered the call of their country. Now more than ever, stories like these must be told...and lessons learned lest we forget, lest we forget.

Someone talking about memories said, "When an older person dies, it is like a library burning down." What some of the youth of Wahama High School accomplished was they kept the library of knowledge of thirty-one veterans from being lost to future generations. How proud will be the children, grandchildren, and those to follow.

These stories and experiences are not for the purpose of glorifying the horrors of war; rather, they are to pay tribute to those who shared and to realize the sacrifices they made for our freedoms. Simply put, "To brighten the future, we must illuminate the past." Lessons learned are lessons kept.

Gratefully,

Hershel Woody Williams
CWO/4, USMC, WWII
Medal of Honor

Iwo Jima, February 23, 1945

Preface

All of this began in 2007. That spring my English 11 class consisted of probably the most talented group of students I have ever taught. Seeking to challenge these pupils, I invited twenty-five guests—members of the local communities ranging in age from sixty-two to ninety-seven—to Wahama High School. I paired each of these senior citizens with one student. After conducting interviews and writing biographies, we proceeded to compile a book called *Voices from around the Bend* about the amazing lives of our guests. With an initial budget of four hundred dollars and a contract with a Tampa, Florida, printing company, we sold nearly four hundred copies—not bad for a group of teenage first-time publishers.

A few months later, I conjured up a different and more expensive publishing idea, this one involving veterans. However, I realized that the prospective costs presented quite a challenge. I pushed the idea to the back of my mind, only to revisit it on occasion, but then in the spring of 2008 I received a call from a friend and past colleague, Teresa Warner. Teresa, a former history teacher, read and loved *Voices from around the Bend* so much that she passed it on to a man named Bruce Darst, head of the American Electric Power River Transportation Division in Lakin, West Virginia. Teresa wanted my next wave of students to write another book, this one about some of the living war veterans of Mason County. Uncannily, she had thought of the same idea as me, which is especially strange considering she and I are polar opposites. Through AEP monies, Mr. Darst agreed to fund the project.

Despite an open invitation in the local newspaper for any interested veterans to contact me regarding participation in this project, I received a grand total of *two* responses. Not wanting to give up on the idea just yet, however, I asked the local VFW's and American Legions for names, and they responded. Word of mouth soon spread as well, and before long I had a lengthy list of veterans to call. As I talked to these men, I found that just about all of them were willing to share their stories. I learned something about veterans from this experience: these men were so humble that very few stepped forward when given the invitation in the newspaper, yet when asked personally, they were elated to oblige. I vividly recall inviting one Vietnam veteran to come to Wahama for an interview. "I've never really talked to anyone about what I did over there," he responded, "but you know what?

Maybe it's about time." Many of the other participants went on to share those same sentiments.

During a four-week time span in March and April of 2009, twenty-seven veterans representing World War II, Korea, Vietnam, and Operation Iraqi Freedom made their way to Wahama for interviews conducted by my junior students; an additional four veterans, unable to physically travel to our school, were visited inside their homes by students. We heard stories that were truly amazing—stories about young men who eagerly volunteered to serve their country in a time of war; stories about the horrors of a battlefield; and stories about how if they could, they would do it all over again for the United States of America. We shared both laughter and tears with these gentlemen as they recalled a bevy of emotional descriptions and accounts, some of which had been recessed in their memories for decades. Talk about an educational experience for twenty-four young high school students!

This compilation of biographic profiles has amounted to a difficult task for both my students and me, but it has been worth it. We've learned a lot along the way. For instance, you know those war heroes that we read about in history books and watch in movies? They're our neighbors, our co-workers, and our family members. They live in Mason County.

On behalf of my students, I want to thank Mr. Darst and everyone at the AEP River Transportation Division for believing in this project and providing us with the financial means to carry it out. Our thanks especially go out to the thirty-one veterans who participated in this book. Some of you by your own admissions re-lived nightmares and fought back tears in order to answer our questions. I pestered you and your family members with phone calls, e-mails, and letters filled with an abundance of requests for the last year. I hope you are proud of the results.

Walter Raynes

Lewis Allen

United States Navy
World War II

By Tory Raynes

Sitting in a gun tub aboard a Merchant Marine ship in the Mediterranean Sea sounds very lonesome and serene—unless, of course, you're in the midst of a violent air-sea battle with live ammunition and explosives bursting all around. For Lewis Allen, this scenario proved all too real as Nazi fire pelted the ship on which he was stationed. While he returned fire, a shell exploded nearby, sending him into the cold sea waters. Fortunately, Allied forces rescued this Point Pleasant resident, who today remembers vividly his naval adventures during World War II.

Allen grew up on a one hundred and fifty-acre farm in Calhoun County, West Virginia. As a teenager, he managed the farm for his parents. However, as World War II erupted, he quickly began to lose his hired hands to the draft. Working on the farm, Allen felt useless to his country, especially with many of his older friends already in the military. As a result, in 1943 on his seventeenth birthday and with his parents' consent, Allen journeyed to Clarksburg, West Virginia, to enlist in the United States Navy. "They were drafting at eighteen, but if you wanted to join sooner, you had to have your parents' signatures," says Allen.

Allen's decision regarding which of the military branches to join was not a tough one. "I had a brother who was in the Army," he says, "and he got discharged because of his bad feet. He told me how tough the infantry was, so I decided to join the Navy instead of the Army. I wasn't going to go through what he had in the Army." After choosing a branch, however, the decisions became more difficult for Allen: "I wasn't all that familiar with the Navy, so I didn't know what to pick as my chosen field. I asked the man at the desk what he would choose if he were me, and he said 'the Armed Guard.' I took his advice, even though I didn't have any idea what the Armed Guard was." Allen soon discovered that the Armed Guard members were gunners that the Navy provided to merchant ships carrying supplies and troops across both the Atlantic and Pacific Oceans during the war.

Upon his departure, Allen reluctantly anticipated six weeks of basic training, but it only lasted four weeks because the Navy at this time rushed its new members through due to the extreme need. Next, Allen traveled to gunnery school in Louisiana for two weeks. There the Navy familiarized him with the types of guns that they expected him to maintain on the merchant ships. From there, Allen received his first ship assignment out of New Orleans and headed to the North Atlantic.

As for his role on a Merchant Marine vessel, Allen states, "The Merchant Marine maintained the ships. They were in charge of the maintenance and the upkeep of the ships." At the war's beginning, German ships and submarines, realizing the importance of these merchant ships, destroyed them in the open seas. As a result, the Navy began to arm these ships with large guns as a means of protection. Allen operated and maintained these guns.

In order to insure the utmost safety, the merchant ships regularly traveled in convoys, with sometimes as many as forty ships to a convoy. Allen recalls that on most occasions the merchant ships were well fortified: "We had depth charges [bombs used by the Navy to defend ships against submerged submarines] all around us and Navy destroyers that served as our escorts. They could detect the enemy submarines when they came within a certain distance, and they would release the depth charges. They would rattle our own ship pretty good."

Allen remembers Liverpool, England, as his ship's destination on his first voyage: "When I first went there in 1944, it was damaged pretty heavily from bombing." From there, it was on to Glasgow, Scotland. "We were taking a variety of things into Army bases. One hold might be full of one thing, and another hold something different. I remember that one of our holds carried big bales of cotton that we had loaded in New Orleans."

Allen says that while on the ship, mail was slow but always seemed to find a way to get to him. "I wrote a lot of letters, but naturally I could never send them off until we came to port," he says. "When we would reach a port, the Navy somehow always made sure that our mail was there waiting for us. I got mostly letters, but one time someone sent me a fruitcake. It was moldy, of course, but I guess it's the thought that counts."

According to Allen, although he seldom feared for his life, he felt many types of stress. For him, the worst part of his job was being out in the middle of the ocean for up to thirty days at a time without seeing any land. "At the beginning, I thought that maybe I had made a grave mistake by volunteering in the Navy," he said. To relieve some of the tension, Allen and his crew mates did various things for pleasure while on the ship, including boxing and playing baseball on the deck.

One of Allen's more memorable voyages began in Philadelphia with the ship making a stop in Virginia to pick up bombs. He laughed, "This is when things got a little scary." Seldom were the ships' crews ever told of their destinations, and this was one of those times. "We ended up going through the Mediterranean Sea, passing the Rock of Gibraltar. Our deck cargo was some Army supplies—Jeeps, trucks and various land equipment." Because of some stormy weather, the ship incurred some heavy damage, and Allen recalls having to dock at a port in North Africa for repairs. The crew disembarked on June 5, 1944, the day before D-Day. "We were all put on alert because of that. Enemy planes were coming across the Mediterranean to help out in Europe, and on the way they would attack our ships."

During this raid, Allen sat in his gun tub, firing at enemy aircraft as they flew overhead. "There were so many ships firing their guns that I really couldn't tell where my rounds were going," he states. Suddenly, a shell exploded near Allen's station, blowing him clear off the ship into the fierce waters of the Mediterranean. "It wasn't quite dark yet, and there was a lot of debris and stuff in the water," he said, recalling the most horrifying experience of his naval career. Allen both thought and worried while floating in the water. "I knew that sooner or later a ship would come for me. What I really worried about, though, was that the sharks would come to me first. It didn't take long for a ship to pull up to me, and I was really happy to hear the crew speaking English. They lowered a ladder off the side to get me in the ship. It turned out to be a British ship, and the crew took me to Italy." There he remained hospitalized for a short time with a leg injury.

While recuperating from his wounds, the Navy assigned Allen to another ship. Upon his hospital release, he boarded the ship, which traversed to Port Said, Egypt, and then through the Suez Canal. "You could only go through it at night," Allen remembers, "because they didn't want the enemy to see who or what was going through it. They feared being bombed." Allen's ship at this time was part of a convoy of about thirty, and the ships had to pass through the canal one at a time. On Christmas Day 1944, his ship sailed through the Red Sea. Its destination was the Tigris River in Iran to unload K-rations.

Allen next sailed to Southeast Africa to pick up coal. After loading the cargo, the crew set off to sea again, this time around the southern tip of Africa with sights set on landing in Sao Paulo, Brazil. After dropping the coal off there, they traveled to Oakland, California. Later, Allen was assigned to a ship headed for the South Pacific. It was at an island base in this area of the world where he and the others aboard the ship heard the news that the war had ended. "There was a lot of celebrating," Allen stated.

After the war's end, however, getting home was a slow process. "Only six gunmen from each ship were allowed to be brought home at a time. There were usually twenty-eight gunners on each one. Luckily, I was among the second set of six called," he recounts. After a quick stop in Guam, Allen found himself stateside in San Francisco. He remembers that upon his return from the South Pacific, the military began the discharge process for the men: "They discharged the men with wives and kids first. Of course, I was single, so I was one of the last." After hanging around San Francisco for a few weeks, Allen finally received that cherished discharge. Next, he hitch-hiked to Shelby, Ohio, where his parents had moved during the war.

Allen eventually made Mason County, West Virginia, his home, working at various places until he settled at Stauffer Chemical Plant, from where he eventually retired. It was in Mason County that he married and raised a family. Sadly, a few years ago while driving a lawn tractor along the side of a road, a car struck Allen, causing serious injuries. Doctors told him that he would never walk again, but this strong-willed man proved them wrong. Today, because of the injuries sustained from the accident, Allen struggles to get from place to place. However, his spirit and faith have brought him a long way from those days sailing on the high seas.

About the Author. Tory Amanda Raynes is a current resident of Mason, West Virginia, where she lives with her father, mother, and younger sister. She is a member of the Wahama varsity cheerleading squad and the choir. In her free time, Tory enjoys writing, cheerleading, and music; however, her favorite hobby is singing. Upon graduation, Tory plans to attend Ohio University to major in dietetics.

World War II veteran Lew Allen poses with student-author Tory Raynes

Paul Ashby

United States Army
Vietnam War

By Miriam Gordon

"When I went to Vietnam, I didn't know what to expect," admits Paul Ashby. However, it didn't take this Army veteran long to become acclimated to his new jungle surroundings in the mid-1960s. In fact, like many of his young American peers, Ashby learned the finer points of being a soldier very quickly.

Ashby graduated from high school in 1965 with intentions of attending college, but after just a few months he decided that the college life did not suit him. He then concluded that joining the Army was what he wanted. "I enlisted because I thought that serving my country was the patriotic thing to do," he says. "I was an energetic, gung-ho kind of kid who wanted to make the best of everything. It was an adventure because I had never done anything like this in my whole life. I was enthusiastic about the whole program." Being an athlete throughout his youth, the intense training during boot camp in Fort Jackson, South Carolina, provided him enjoyment.

Although he remembers his instructors vividly, one who took Ashby under his wing stands out in particular.

With the aid of this instructor, Ashby, then nineteen, soon rose to the top of his class, and his superiors nominated him for Officer's Candidate School at Fort Belvoir, Virginia, just south of Washington, D.C. Here, Ashby took part in Engineering OCS. For twenty-two of the twenty-four weeks of this schooling, he and his fellow officer candidates trained in Quantico, Virginia, a Marine base. During this time, a confidence course provided him with his greatest challenge. "It was raining, and I was climbing a huge ladder made of logs, and I fell," he recalls. This accident resulted in two broken ribs. "Because of this," he continued, "they wanted to recycle me back to the thirteenth week of training, which was when things got really tough. I decided no way was I going back." Three weeks later, Ashby received orders dispatching him to Vietnam.

Once in this part of war-torn Southeast Asia, the Army stationed him inside the city of Saigon. Ashby says, "The city was so foreign to me; I guess I was in a mystique of sorts." During this time, he volunteered to serve at a post office delivering mail into one of the most dangerous parts of the city, Highway 13. "Being young and sort of full of the military itself, I didn't see any danger in it." This lasted about four months.

Afterward, the Army transferred Ashby to the Cambodian border with the first infantry division. As a combat engineer, he could do anything from implementing demolition to using heavy equipment. His job often consisted of taking a mine sweep team into the jungles and clearing fifteen miles of road per day. Ashby states, "We were supported by infantry every morning when we went out, and there were lots of firefights. We often got ambushed, and I saw lots of casualties." The worst casualties, Ashby recalls, were natives in the villages. "We would take our mine sweep crews into the villages looking for weapons or explosives, and the civilian casualties were the ones who affected you the most." Ashby particularly remembers a pair of dead ten-year-old twin girls killed by combat fire. It had been the first time that he had seen twins while in Vietnam, and unfortunately it had to be under very morbid circumstances.

As for the emotions that he felt while in Vietnam, Ashby says that he was scared every single day. "Anybody that was over there that says they weren't scared, I don't think they're being very honest," he said. As an example of one specific frightening memory, he remembers a terrifying night at camp. Ashby was on guard duty outside of the perimeter fence with only a radio and a pistol. With the moon lighting some of his surroundings, he briefly made out the silhouettes of the enemy that surrounded him. They illuminated the sky with flares, and for a moment Ashby caught glimpses of enemy soldiers with machine guns only fifteen feet from him. While hiding behind a small bush, he prayed. This, according to Ashby, is when he really came to know the Lord.

As for other recollections, Ashby remembers being very distant in regards to his family during his time in Vietnam; therefore, he did not communicate with them much. Along the lines of food, Ashby says that just about everything he ate came from a can, otherwise known as C-rations. "I learned to eat cold spaghetti along with cold ham and eggs. We didn't have anything to heat it up with." He also recalls having very few supplies. "We had a rifle and two uniforms. You also had to make sure your boots were always dry, especially during monsoon season, because you could get jungle rot, where your feet actually started to decay. It was therefore important to have clean socks."

Twice while in the service, Ashby received time for R and R, or rest and relaxation. Once the Army sent him to Australia, and he also received liberty

Jerry Bain

United States Marine Corps
Vietnam War

By Taylor Hysell

During the Vietnam War thousands of men put their own lives on the line for their country. Many were drafted and didn't have a choice but to go to Vietnam to do their tours. One tour, however, wasn't quite enough for Jerry Bain, who twice traversed across the Pacific and engaged in numerous operations, including Operation Swift, one of the bloodiest assaults in the war.

Jerry Bain was your typical kid. He grew up with four brothers and a sister in Illinois, where he enjoyed riding his bike, playing baseball, shooting basketball, and swimming wherever he found water. Being a teenager, Bain disliked school but reluctantly attended anyway, graduating from high school in 1966. Soon after, the Army drafted him, but Bain didn't want to be in the Army. Therefore, he attempted to enlist in the Navy, but they declined to accept him, citing that he had already been drafted. Next, Bain tried the Marine Corps; they accepted him, and before he knew it, he found himself on the fast track to Vietnam, where he spent a total of twenty-six months.

Bain made a difficult decision to wait and tell his family that he was leaving until the day before he was to depart for basic training. Bain recalls, "My mother was very upset, and even though my father didn't show it, he was upset also. At the time though, he just told me to be careful." When Bain arrived at training in San Diego, California, a man approached, telling him that he belonged with him, and since he was the first one there, it was his job to stand outside and wait for everyone and collect their record books. Being an obedient Marine on his first day, Bain followed orders, waiting for four hours before being permitted to join the others. "The training experience is very mind-breaking and mind-boggling," said Bain. "They break you and all your respect down and then they build you back up, and it's hard to handle." Another excruciating task during his eight weeks of boot camp was taking an abundance of tests. "There was no way to prepare for them; you just took them and by how you did on them was how they put everyone into categories," Bain confesses. "Boot camp was one of the hardest things I've had to do."

At just the young age of twenty, Bain served his first tour in Vietnam. He remembers it as scary and hot. Despite knowing nothing about the country, he remained determined to do what he could because he wanted to serve his country. When Bain completed his first tour, he came out a corporal but returned a sergeant. Bain carried the radio for his company and experienced an abundance of combat as part of seventeen different operations.

"Food and personal hygiene were not very good there," said Bain. He and his fellow Marines mostly ate outdated C-rations that proved unsatisfying. Oftentimes, they welcomed rain because it provided a method of getting clean. Cleanliness could also be gained by bathing in creeks, but Bain recalls paying the consequences for this because he would then have to pick the leeches off of his body when he got out. Needless to say, combat Marines lived very uncomfortably in the Vietnamese jungles.

A typical day out of the brush for Bain consisted of writing, talking, listening to the radio, cleaning weapons, playing games, sleeping, maintaining personal hygiene, and various other simple tasks. "We always had to stay alert and constantly be on our toes," he says. A typical day in the brush, however, was a completely different story. In addition to worrying about the Vietcong, the fear of snakes tormented the men. "I was always very hot and just put one foot in front of the other," Bain laughs. Carrying one hundred and forty pounds of equipment and supplies on his back compounded matters. Being the radio man, he hauled the radio, extra batteries and other radio supplies (which he was responsible for), along with socks, pants, shirts, shaving gear, personal hygiene gear, enough meals for one or two weeks, and three or four canteens of water, which the men often poured Kool-Aid in for flavor. They also added iodine tablets to kill the germs. The Marines often slept in the dirt and fretted about large mosquitoes.

Every time Bain had to go out he carried his good luck charm with him—a green Bible. According to Bain, it worked well when he took part in Operation Swift. During this operation, the participating Marines walked right into an L-shaped ambush, forcing Bain to jump over and lie beside a rice paddy dike. Bain continued his story: "Then I saw one of the North Vietnamese step up on the dike and spray the area down, and that's when I got shot in the back. The bullet went through my gas mask and my spare radio battery and stopped just before it got to my radio. I wasn't even aware of it until they had to throw gas out, and when I reached to get my mask, I felt holes everywhere. That's when I knew the Man upstairs was looking down after me."

That was the only place he was hit, and the bullet stopped just before it hit his radio, so they luckily still had communication. During that same time Bain's artillery operator had lain there all night while the Vietnamese stripped him of his clothes, equipment, and radio. Ironically, a freak accident occurred thirty days later when the two sides fought again right outside of the Marine base. During the battle, they recovered their same radio there, and all they had to do was change the frequencies. The next day Bain and his Marines turned back the enemy and took over fifty-three POW's. Those are just a few of the difficult situations in which Bain found himself, and they impacted him greatly.

During his tours in Vietnam, Bain's unit suffered numerous casualties and witnessed many horrible incidents. "One of the saddest things that you would have to do was carry a body off to the chopper," said Bain. He still wakes up in cold sweats and remembers how he carried a fallen friend for the last time. In an attempt to look at the positive side, Bain said that the war did not consist of all bad things though, because he learned a lot about dealing with intense situations, and he feels like it helped him grow into a man. He now respects his government more and loves his country.

When Bain returned home, he started a normal life with his wife Karen, who he has now been married to for forty years. He met her on leave while in Point Pleasant with a friend from the war, who is now his brother-in-law. Bain is a family man and has one daughter. Today, he proudly belongs to many veterans' organizations, including the American Legion, VFW, and AMVETS. He also enjoys helping disabled or disadvantaged veterans, such as transporting them to the hospital.

On March 26, 1999, a friend of Bain's emailed him, writing that she thought she knew someone from India 3/5, Bain's company in Vietnam. Thinking that this man, Curtis Eidson, had died in battle, it surprised Bain to find out otherwise some thirty years later. Upon communicating with one another, the two men decided to locate as many of their company buddies as possible with hopes of having a reunion. Later that same year, a small amount of the 3/5 gathered in Georgia. Now a decade later, the reunion has grown enormously and takes place the first week of June in South Carolina, where around 475 people attend. In addition to cooking their own food and telling a plethora of stories, they pick a name of a fallen fellow Marine and contact his family in order to honor him. Four families they previously contacted still come back every year and love what they do. "It's just a great thing where everyone can get together and enjoy themselves and the company of others," said Bain.

Many people are unaware that Bain was instrumental in bringing the traveling version of the Vietnam Wall to Point Pleasant a few years ago. He worked hard for three years and underwent a long process but felt like every minute was worth it in the end. An estimated 35,000 people came from all over the region.

Outwardly, Jerry Bain wears the scars of the Vietnam War very well. He remains active in many activities and maintains a very positive outlook regarding life. It is often difficult for people to realize the extreme perils that Vietnam brought upon young men like Bain, but all of us owe a tremendous amount of gratitude to all the Jerry Bain's who defended the beliefs and freedoms of our Nation.

About the author. Taylor Hysell and her family are residents of New Haven, West Virginia. She is the daughter of Jason and Lisa Hysell and has one younger brother, Derek. She is a member of the Wahama High School girl's basketball and softball teams. Besides playing sports, she enjoys hanging out with her friends, watching movies, and listening to music. Taylor is also a member of the National Honor Society. As for the athlete's future plans, she wants to attend West Virginia University and specialize in the medical field.

Jerry Bain spent a total of twenty-six months in Vietnam. Among his recent accomplishments include helping to bring the traveling Vietnam Wall to Point Pleasant a few years ago.

James Ball

United States Navy
World War II

By Tiffanie Miller

The worst of nightmares that awaken most people pale in comparison to the real, ghastly horror experienced by James Ball in October 1944. As a yeoman striker on the Navy ship *USS Gambier Bay*, Ball found himself among numerous crew members struggling for life in the middle of the vast Pacific Ocean after abandoning ship during a Japanese attack. His story of survival is truly amazing.

As a Navy selective volunteer in June 1943, the then-nineteen-year-old Ball's war experience began in the Pacific Ocean aboard the *Gambier Bay* about a year and a half after his enlistment. Ball, however, was not officially a member of the ship's company; instead, he was a part of the air squadron (VC-10) attached to the ship.

On October 25, 1944, Ball experienced the most horrific event of his life. According to his accounts, he was awakened early that morning by general quarters call. Ball remembers it being a misty morning, gray and overcast. Each man had a station, and they were told to go to them. Ball was an air plotter, a collector of information on incoming aircraft. "As I settled into my station, I heard a pilot report the sighting of unidentified ships," recalls Ball. "The pilot radioed that there were four battleships, eight cruisers, and eleven destroyers only twenty miles away, closing in at thirty knots." The pilot had made what was called a "dry run" and drew fire. After this, all pilots rushed to get their planes launched. In a hurry, some of the planes launched without being completely refueled and without being armed with bombs. By this time, according to Ball, the Japanese were getting close enough to fire salvoes.

The Japanese started firing and the captain could tell the next salvo would hit their ship, so he ordered that they take zigzag courses in hopes of throwing off the Japanese. However, after they zigzagged several times, the

Japanese found the range and fired a salvo, hitting the forward engine room and putting them at a dead stop in the water.

After that, the ship just sat there as each salvo fired direct hits. Ball said, "I was so scared that I was afraid to move, and my face felt like it was on fire." In addition, Ball had not eaten since the night before. He remembers one of his shipmates saying that he was going to the port side to see what was going on. Although Ball attempted to convince him to stay, the young man refused.

"We were under attack for about two hours," recounts Ball. The order to abandon the ship finally came at approximately 8:50 am. "The first thing we did was check out our life belts and jackets. After the order to abandon the ship, all I had to do was go through the hatchway on the starboard side, and from there I could get over the side of the ship." The crew took turns climbing down the rope. Ball said, "It felt like someone was sitting on my shoulders while I climbed down." By nine o'clock, just ten minutes after the order to abandon ship, the *Gambier Bay* sank underwater.

After Ball reached the water, he swam towards the ship's stern. As he passed under the motor whaleboat, it got hit and blew up. He and five others continued swimming towards the stern. Luckily, someone had cut a floating net from the ship, so Ball and the others used this to hang onto.

When the survivors reached a safe distance from the ship, they climbed on the net, exhausted and vomiting from all of the salt water swallowed. "There were several explosions, and pieces of the ship's deck boards would come through the air towards us," he said. Some of the timbers were used by survivors on which to cling. After a short time, Ball remembers a Japanese destroyer went by in what seemed like full speed. "We worried that they were going to see us and fire on the net that we were on, so we flattened it out and acted like we were dead."

Throughout the day more survivors joined their net. Some floated on rafts, while others hung onto pieces of wood. None of them had any food or water for two days. Those who ventured to drink the seawater became delirious. "Some would say that they were going for a beer, going ashore, or even that they saw their relatives waving at them," states Ball. "Many of the men were wounded with face and upper body burns."

The second day was hot, clear, and bright. Almost all of the men suffered from sunburn by noon that day. Some of them died. While one of them would say a few words in tribute, the others would bury the dead at sea.

Perhaps the most terrifying part of the entire ordeal was the sharks. While abandoned crewmen drifted at night, they could see the vicious predators swimming around them. They feared that the sharks would attack them, and they often did. Mostly, the sharks fed on the stragglers though.

All told, one hundred and sixteen men died at sea from the wounds and sharks. Ball recalls one occurrence he experienced with a shipmate: "He had a back injury and was unable to keep his head out of the water. I tried to hold it up for him. He kept drifting in and out of consciousness and asking 'Where are the rescue ships?'" Ball said he constantly tried to give the suffering man words of encouragement, like "It won't be long," and "They will be coming soon."

Sometime in the morning of October 27th, the survivors were picked up by an LCI, a type of military landing craft, sent out by the Seventh Fleet. The ship steered along the side of them, taking the most seriously wounded on board first. By noon they reached the decision that all of the survivors had been rescued; they then set course for San Pedro on Leyte. "I remember having the strength to climb up the rope ladder, where they got a hold of my hands," says Ball. "Then I was helped the rest of the way. I remember standing on my feet, and then I collapsed. I don't know how long I was out, but the next thing I remember, someone gave me black coffee."

Ball mentioned that the LCI left the Leyte Gulf and traveled by an LST, a landing craft, back to New Guinea, and from there they transferred to the *SS Lureline*, another ship. They then departed New Guinea and started home by way of Brisbane, Australia.

When Ball boarded the *SS Lureline*, he went to the hospital to see who was there. The shipmate that he had tried to talk out of going to the port side of the *Gambier Bay* was lying there. He had one of his legs missing, and Ball said the first thing the man said to him was, "I should have listened to you."

Ball says, "As I look back to the time of the sinking of the *USS Gambier Bay* and all the bad memories of that awful day, I thank my God for guiding me through all of it. Praise Him forever." To this day, the attack of American ships in the Gulf of Leyte by Japanese battleships and cruisers remains one of the greatest naval victories in U.S. military history. "The American battle group consisted of just six small carriers, and all the protection these small carriers had were a screen of destroyers and destroyer escorts around us," said Ball. "Because of this battle, the Japanese battle group never attacked the landing battle group in Leyte Gulf," he concluded.

About the Author. Tiffanie Miller, born January 19, 1992, is a current resident of Hartford, West Virginia. She attends Wahama High School and is the daughter of Stephanie Jarrell and Steve Miller. Tiffanie comes from a large family of three sisters and two brothers. She plans on attending college after high school and going into the medical field.

*James Ball served as a yeoman striker during World War II
aboard the USS Gambier Bay.*

Richard Broadwater

United States Army
Vietnam War

By Hannah Foreman

Although anyone who has ever traveled by air probably considered the repercussions of a crash landing, very few people, thankfully, have ever experienced a tragedy of such magnitude. However, this was not the case for Richard Broadwater during his tour in Vietnam. Broadwater, a helicopter machine gunner, was involved in not one, but three aircraft crashes. These incidents as well as others have contributed to some very vivid memories for Broadwater in regard to his war experience.

Like most twenty-year-old males in the 1960's, Broadwater felt young and invincible. He graduated high school and planned on pursuing a career in automotives. When the year 1966 arrived, America had already joined the Vietnam War, which suddenly interrupted all of Broadwater's plans. Instead of resenting the country's involvement in the war, Broadwater did what any true lover of his or her nation would—sign up for the draft. He describes that day as nothing out of the ordinary: "I simply did my duty as a fit, healthy boy." After a few months passed, Broadwater received a letter from Uncle Sam calling his name.

Up until then, Broadwater lived with his mother and older brother, whom the military drafted around the same time. Broadwater tells of their mother's compliant emotions: "It was hard to leave our mother, but I think she understood that her boys were needed somewhere else." Broadwater wrote to his mother once a week, and the souvenirs he sent her let her know that his heart remained at home in West Virginia. Another reason why Broadwater never hesitated to answer the call is that he had not settled down yet to begin a family. However, fighting for his country made him want to do just that. This wise-from-experience soldier also realized how much he valued and appreciated everything he once took for granted.

At the time of Broadwater's draft, he recalls, "The Army was calling out men like crazy." He feels this is the reason his basic training didn't last long. "The Army wasn't looking for men; they just wanted bodies," he states on the

Broadwater, the memories live on in his mind of a youthful time when he served his country well.

About the Author: Hannah Elizabeth Foreman, a seventeen-year-old senior at Wahama High School, has lived in New Haven her entire life. She is involved in many extra-curricular activities, such as band and all-state choir. Hannah also enjoys her after-school job at the local Health Aid Pharmacy. She is currently the president of her school's chapter of the National Honor Society and ranked first in her class. Her future plans include attending a university to pursue a career in either criminal justice or medical research.

In Vietnam, Richard Broadwater routinely flew in helicopter missions. Unfortunately, he crashed on three occasions.

Harold Bumgarner

United States Army
World War II

By Zach Jividen

Harold Bumgarner is a very talented individual. From his organization of gospel music events to his beautiful landscape paintings, this eighty-eight-year-old has long been an icon in Mason County's Bend Area. However, many years ago Bumgarner's talent consisted of setting up communication systems through France and Germany as Allied forces advanced into Europe during the later years of World War II.

In August of 1942, Bumgarner, after getting drafted into the Army, took a preliminary physical exam in Point Pleasant. After passing, around twenty men from Mason County hopped onto a bus headed for Huntington, West Virginia, where they were evaluated and sworn into the Army. Bumgarner admits that he really never intended on going into the military. "I didn't have any objections toward the service. I just didn't want to go in," he states. Like many of his fellow Americans, however, when Uncle Sam called, he answered with no resistance.

The then-twenty-one-year-old Mason Countian had never been out of West Virginia much, so he naturally anticipated his departure overseas with some trepidation. "We left New York on a big ship after dark. I went to sleep, and when I woke up the next morning, I went up on the deck and saw nothing but water. There was no land in sight. I prayed to the Lord then and told Him, 'If you get me through this, then I'll be a good person.'"

When he disembarked the ship, Bumgarner stepped onto the beaches in North Africa. His camp was located on a high hill in the town of Algiers, a North African city in the country of Algeria, where many Allied troops were stationed. "That's where Allied forces' headquarters were located," says Bumgarner. "General Eisenhower had his main office in Algiers."

Bumgarner was a member of the Army Signal Corps, a company that installed telephones, switchboards, and lines. "The company was made up of all telephone people. We could put a telephone anywhere," he stated. He had gained much of his expertise in this skill in the fall of 1942 at Camp Crowder, Missouri. He recalls having the most fun learning to climb the poles, using what he called "linemen's spurs." Bumgarner's newly assigned duties actually came as a surprise. At the time of his being drafted, he admits that he was unaware that not all soldiers toted guns and fought in combat.

When Bumgarner first arrived in Algiers, however, his main responsibilities came as a guard and corporal of the guard. One of his chief duties as corporal of the guard consisted of scheduling the men for their turns on guard duty— two hours on, and four hours off. Although today Bumgarner appears extremely mild mannered and easy-going, he apparently had an ornery side in the 1940's, for he recounted a story of how he once taught a young guard under his charge a valuable lesson: "After I put him on his post, I decided that he needed to be frightened in order to understand the seriousness of guarding the camp at night. As I hid around the corner from where he was about to walk, I noticed him half asleep. When he came near enough, I grabbed his rifle. He was surprised and emotionally shocked, but he got the point."

After a few months of time in North Africa, the Army transferred Bumgarner and the others in his company to Naples, Italy. They departed Algiers on a liberty ship, a slow cargo vessel. After a one-night stop in Augusta, Sicily, they arrived in Naples, where troops were being loaded into ships in preparation for taking southern France. This was about three months after the D-Day invasion. Bumgarner himself sailed to France in September 1944 after a thirty-day stay in Italy.

Once in Lyon, France, Bumgarner again found his talents unutilized, as he found himself doing very little at first. He remembers being ordered to dig a lot of trenches, but soon German POW's took his place, and he was thankful for it. However, Bumgarner's luck soon changed. A Lieutenant Novack was commissioned to assemble a crew of telephone technicians to install switchboards into semi trailers. "Telephone communication was absolutely necessary," he says. "They couldn't depend on the radio because the Germans would pick up the signals." One day after speaking to Novack about his artistic talents, Bumgarner was asked to create drawings of all the mechanical layouts and records of materials used. His drawings later formed the contents of a small booklet that served as a manual for future reference purposes. This was one of the most enjoyable moments that Bumgarner experienced in his military life.

Bumgarner finally was able to put his telephone training to use. As Allied troops stormed through France and into Germany, Bumgarner's company followed close behind. "We had to restore all the telephone communications, and sometimes we just added to the lines that were already there. There was a lot of overhead work with cables, yet some of the work was with underground cables."

In March 1945, just after the Battle of the Bulge, Bumgarner's company moved into Germany. He vividly recalls some of the smaller cities he passed through, such as Saarbucken and Kaiserslautern. It was in the latter city where he remembers him and his buddies taking three German rifles that they had found into the woods for a little fun. "We suddenly heard someone yell, 'Hold your fire, hold your fire,'" explains Bumgarner. "It was an American Colonel who had been up there in the woods. He gave us quite a butt-chewing."

About a month later, the battalion moved on to the city of Heidelburg. While here, Bumgarner and his company learned of the German surrender. "It was mainly like a big relief," said Bumgarner when asked what it had been like to hear the news. "There weren't any celebrations, at least not where I was." Bumgarner mentioned, however, that by this time everyone knew that the surrender was coming. "For the longest time, Allied airplanes had filled the sky bombing all the major cities and industrial places. Those planes and bombers just completely annihilated all the industries. There is no way that Germany could have continued to survive that."

Bumgarner experienced a lot of contact with German civilians, and he liked them very much. "They were great people. You'd think your enemy would be trying to kill you all the time, but they weren't. They were all people who were skilled and knew crafts—cabinet-makers, ironworkers—you name it, they could do it. In fact, they did a lot of our work." Bumgarner mentioned that many of the Germans were opposed to the Nazis and hated Hitler but were somewhat powerless. "They were just victims of the circumstances."

After twenty-two months overseas, Bumgarner finally came home in 1945. Amazingly though, after the war had ended in Europe, it took him six months to get home. "I was in non-combat service, and they took the men who had the most dangerous duties and brought them back first," he remembers. While waiting his turn, he lived in three different tent camps. He stated that the best part of his overseas experience was getting to see all the different places. "It was all a big adventure to me. I was enlightened to see how other people lived, their religious beliefs, and the way they made a living."

Finally, on November 15, 1945, Bumgarner sailed out of Marseille, France. He was coming home. Arriving in Long Island, New York, nine days later in the night, Bumgarner remembers seeing a large sign lit up that read, "Welcome Home Boys, Job Well Done." He later was sent to Fort Meade, Maryland, to complete his military service. Shortly after, he returned home to the New Haven area, where he still resides today, and married his wife, Naomi.

Throughout the years Bumgarner has maintained a very productive life. He continued using his artistic talents for many years, creating several paintings. In addition, he and Naomi have been instrumental in organizing and helping with local gospel sings.

Aside from basic training and a little tomfoolery with some German guns, Harold Bumgarner never fired a weapon during World War II, nor did the enemy ever fire upon him. Yet he and thousands of other members of the military support services carried an awesome responsibility. Whereas the infantry began the liberating process of Europe from the Nazi regime, men like Bumgarner completed it. Today, he looks back on his years in the Army with great honor and pride, as well he should.

About the author: Gibbstown resident Zachary Jividen is a senior at Wahama High School. He enjoys driving around and hanging out with his girlfriend and spending time with his parents, Barry Jividen and Dawn Stephens. Always talking, Zachary has never had a dull moment in his whole seventeen years of life. Zachary said, "Interviewing a hero like Harold Bumgarner was a once-in-a-lifetime experience."

Harold Bumgarner utilized his artistic talents to create drawings of mechanical layouts and records of materials while in the European Theater.

Japanese. They would hit the tops of the trees that they were in and just take the tops of the trees out."

This Marine's division was set to take control and clear every last fox hole and bunker across an assigned mountain. While taking this area, Gibbs was a rifleman in the Fleet Marine Force, which put him in the front line of battle. The night before they took the mountain, the Japanese soldiers drank an alcoholic beverage called saki and then would try to fight the next day. This left his group to just wait in their fox holes and take advantage of the drunken enemy. "It was just an unbelievable experience. They made easy targets because they would just charge in a straight line right toward our fox holes."

On July 2, 1944, just a little after two weeks of battle, Gibbs and a buddy took cover behind a bunker that soon drew heavy enemy fire. "We decided to move over next to this big rock, just about five feet away. Just then a shell exploded from where we had moved. I thought at the time that I had gone blind." Luckily, however, Gibbs' vision remained in tact. Shrapnel, though, entered his hand, shoulder, and leg. After yelling "bacon and eggs" (their code words meaning help), he and his partner were transported by jeep to a field hospital in order to recover. Gibbs spent a week in the field hospital, and then caught up with his outfit to continue fighting.

"Many people would surprise you," stated Gibbs, when recounting a story about a man that rarely talked until the day the Japanese brought tanks toward them. Gibbs remembers the quiet guy running up to the tanks and throwing grenades down in the pilot holes.

Gibbs and his division remained on Saipan until the day the Japanese surrendered. "It was the happiest day of my life knowing they surrendered," he said. Soon after this, his division occupied Nagasaki, where the atomic bomb exploded. Gibbs recalls the devastated city looking like "black soot."

After twenty-seven months in the Marines, Gibbs received his honorable discharge and the Purple Heart in Bainbridge, Maryland. He then returned home, going to work for American Electric Power and marrying the love of his life, Gerri. Today, in addition to his wife, Gibbs boasts of three daughters—Carol Lathey, Sharon Lloyd, and Carletta Holbrook—and eighteen grandchildren and great-grandchildren. He also thanks God for every day that he lives and for protecting him on a desolate, unknown island where he came so close to dying sixty-five years ago. For these reasons, he will continue for the rest of his life to sing those songs of praise.

About the Author. Terry Henry, whose father and grandfather go by the same name, is the son of Shelly Henry and older brother to Macy, Aaron, Blake, and Brogan. A senior at Wahama, this Mason resident enjoys participating on the high school baseball team and being amongst his friends. He also enjoys working out at the local fitness center.

U.S. Marine Carl Gibbs saw heavy combat on the island of Saipan during World War II. Pictured with him from left are daughter Carletta, wife Gerri, and daughters Sharon and Carol.

Frank Gilkey

United States Marine Corps
Vietnam War

By Tim Roush

Like so many of his fellow Marines who served in Vietnam, Frank Gilkey looks upon his tour of duty with a variety of emotions. Although honored to serve the United States in Vietnam, he counts it as the worst time of his life. Even though he holds no regrets concerning his enlistment in the Marine Corps, he was never happier than the moment his plane left Danang, ending his tour. Unfortunately for Gilkey and so many other Vietnam veterans, the tribulations of war still live on in their memories.

Born in Biloxi, Mississippi, sixty-three years ago soon after World War II ended, Gilkey came from a military family. Since his father served in the Army Air Corps, Gilkey was born on a base. However, his family soon moved to the country just outside of Jackson, Ohio. When he reached adulthood, Gilkey says, "I was at that place in life where everyone was asking me what I was going to do. After high school, I really had no plans or dreams. I saw this Marine recruiter and signed up for a term of four years.

"When I enlisted, I or nobody really my age had ever heard of Vietnam. I was in boot camp before I even heard anyone mention the word," says Gilkey. Yet after boot camp at Parris Island, the Southeast Asian country was his destination for a total of thirteen months. Gilkey's age was twenty at the time. "It was thirteen *long* months," Gilkey stresses. "That was the regular tour of duty."

When Gilkey first discovered that he would be dispatched to Vietnam, he felt extremely apprehensive. "I didn't really know what was going on there. I had no idea. When you're twenty, you get the feeling that you're invincible, but as the time to go approached, reality set in, and the scarier it became." Instead of fearing enemy bullets, however, Gilkey sensed more fear about being so far away from home. "It was a long way to go for a country boy," he says.

Gilkey's first stop in Vietnam was a small camp outside the town of Chu Lai. He recalls it being near the most beautiful beach he has ever seen. "My buddies and I didn't have much free time, but we did make our way occasionally to the beach to swim. It was a nice release." Gilkey said that music provided another outlet for the Marines. However, he conceded, "If you did what you were supposed to do, you had hardly any free time."

Gilkey was attached to an air wing unit. "It was actually a radar squadron," he says. "We did a lot of the air flight routines." As a radio operator, he helped maintain radio contact. Chu Lai was a major airport that contained fighter jets and three helicopter units. "Constantly, the helicopters went in and out." The main purpose of these helicopters consisted of daily transporting troops in and out of combat zones. In addition, there were many Hueys, or gunship helicopters, on the base. "The sound of helicopters flip me out even today," says Gilkey. His worst recollection of them was that they often left early in the morning with vibrant young men and returned in the evening with some of the same men in body bags. "I felt glad that I didn't have to serve in the war in that capacity," states Gilkey, "but in a way it made me feel guilty, and it still haunts me."

As a radio operator, Gilkey recalls arising very early each morning, just a little before daylight, in fact. After a shower, morning formation, and duty assignments, a plethora of jobs awaited. Among the ones Gilkey remembers most are maintaining the radios and using them to keep in constant radio contact with the helicopters and men in the field. Other common tasks included digging latrines and picking up trash. "We would put our trash in these big cans and dump them outside the compound, and people would come and actually fight over our garbage. They were pretty desperate people. It's no wonder they were so messed up," he recalls.

A typical day for Gilkey often consisted of guard duty. He often performed this on the side of a hill; the other side contained bunkers and wires. "We were protected by the side of a hill, but then we had our main line on the other side, where we had big lights. In fact, we had electricity all the time. You'd often see shadows out in the distance from the lights, and your imagination would play tricks on you. It was very frightening." In addition to the shadows, mortars often exploded, or flares came down. Gilkey admits, though, that in spite of these small fears, his unit really experienced very little trouble compared to other Americans.

Gilkey stated that throughout his entire thirteen months in Vietnam, he never at any time felt one hundred-percent safe. "From the time my feet got out of the plane to the time I left, I was absolutely terrified. I have never lived with fear like I did there." Gilkey says that one reason for such fright rested in the difficulty of identifying the enemy. "We couldn't even fully trust the lady that was doing our laundry." Gilkey recalls many civilians being allowed on the base, but the Marines could never be absolutely sure about where their loyalties lay. He said that he and his unit continually carried their weapons and were always ready to shoot someone if necessary.

Gilkey and the others in his unit had a significant amount of contact with the Vietnamese civilians. "We went on what they called 'Civic Action Patrols.' We took doctors and nurses to go to treat the people. I would often give the kids some of the things that my parents sent me." The Vietnamese were extremely poor and had very little. "I'd take toothbrushes, toothpaste, soap, and other different toiletries, and the kids would fight over that stuff. They would literally gang you for it."

One other interesting incident involving a Vietnamese national stands out in Gilkey's mind. It took place at a small naval detachment that served as a hospital. During his three-month stay, he frequently noticed a Vietnamese man with a bandage around his foot. He also spoke English very well. "I asked him what was wrong with him, and he said that he had been born with a club foot. The hospital there operated on him several times and made his foot improved on each occasion. They finally got him one hundred percent better, and he left. We didn't hear from him again until one day they killed him for trying to infiltrate through our lines. We spent all that time and money to cure him, and he turned out to be a V.C."

Gilkey recognizes the poverty of the people as one of the biggest problems regarding Vietnam. "We were trying to preserve the deplorable lifestyle they already had, and the Communists kept promising a better way to live," he says. "The Communists would lie to them about free land and things like that." He recalls many of the Vietnamese creating makeshift homes out of old pieces of metal draped over tree limbs, as well as cardboard shacks. "They used anything to get out of the heat. Sometimes people in the U.S. think they have it bad. They don't have it anything like those people."

Staying in contact with family posed few if any problems for Gilkey, as free postage allowed him to write home just about every day. "I tried to tell them how things were going every single day, but some things I didn't want to tell." Phones were not available, except for emergencies, and they could only be accessed through the Red Cross. He continued by saying, "We were very isolated and didn't really know much about what was going on at home."

When his tour finally ended, Gilkey recalls it was at that time the highlight of his life. He said, "You would fly out of Danang on a commercial Continental Golden jet." Once aboard, Gilkey remembers that when he saw a stewardess, he thought about her being the first American girl he had seen in thirteen months. "When that jet lifted off and we were off Vietnamese soil, the whole plane erupted with spontaneous cheering, and I don't think there was a dry eye on the whole plane. That crushing weight was gone for all of us, and it was a great feeling." When they got back to the States, armed guards boarded the plane and wouldn't let them get off. Gilkey isn't sure, but he thinks there was a war demonstration going on, and the guards were only on board for their protection. "It really bothered me," he said. "Here I was, a soldier who risked his life for over a year. I land in the States, and I'm treated like a criminal. One thing's for sure—it wasn't a hero's welcome." Gilkey then served the rest of his military tenure in California.

As for today, Gilkey recently retired from American Electric Power. The Point Pleasant resident enjoys the company of his loving wife, Lynda, along with his children and grandchildren. He can often be found fishing at one of his favorite spots or attending the First Baptist Church in Mason, where he remains very active.

About the Author. Timothy Roush was born and raised in West Virginia in the country. He is the son of Timmy and Rene Roush from West Columbia, West Virginia, where he attends Wahama High School and the Mason County Career Center, to train in either machine tool or welding. Upon graduation, he plans on further training to become a machinist or a boilermaker.

Mason County for the Middle East, but first a two and a half month training session at Fort Dix, New Jersey ensued.

Like most soldiers, leaving family behind, especially his four-year-old son Braden, provided Gray with the most difficult facet of leaving. Gray described his mother as not necessarily shocked by the news but somewhat overwhelmed. "She kept asking, 'What do you need me to do? What about Braden?'" Gray, a single father, admits that it was difficult to explain the situation to Braden, and that over the few weeks preceding his departure, he tried to gradually prepare his son for what was happening.

In February of 2004, the members of the 3664th MC finally found themselves on a plane headed for Kuwait, where they would then travel by truck into Iraq. According to Gray, it helped tremendously to be heading into a war zone with men and women in whom he was already familiar. "It was a big advantage, in my opinion. We all felt comfortable around one another. Many of the reserve units in Iraq were piecemealed together, but I was with people that I had known for twenty years."

Once in Iraq, the men traveled via a convoy of trucks to Fallujah, a key city in the early part of Operation Iraqi Freedom. Gray recalls that even though his family had no idea of his exact location in the war-torn nation, his son seemed to sense it all along. "Braden snuck around watching the war on television and saw the reports about the violence in Fallujah," states Gray. "He told everyone that that was where I was, and it turned out he was right." Gray frequently received opportunities to call Braden, but often it was discomforting for the youngster. "One time during a phone call to him, we got mortared," he says. "Another time, a rocket attack started while I talked to him."

Gray played a major role in the operations involving the 3664th MC while in Iraq. As a Readiness NCO, he made sure that the unit was travel-ready before ever even leaving for the Middle East. Once at Fort Dix, he was re-assigned to a platoon sergeant position. One of his main roles included operating a communications center—they called it an Internet Café—for the troops so that they could maintain contact with loved ones back home. "We started out with twenty laptop computers and four phones and remained open 24/7," he says. In addition to overseeing this communication network, he oversaw a security detail in the LSA, which was responsible for supervising the Iraqi workers and foreign contractors. He and his soldiers were in charge of keeping these people safe and secure.

Although enemy fire did not occur on an everyday basis, there were plenty of moments when Gray and his fellow troops came under attack. "It consisted mainly of mortar and rocket attacks," he said. He vividly recalls one particular situation that provided a close call: "One night I was outside checking on security detail. There were three of us standing on a small berm just talking, and all of a sudden we saw a flash followed by an explosion not too far from us. It knocked all three of us to the ground. We scrambled to get all the men to safety, which we did." The ironic part of this story is that sometime later, Gray and his friends discovered that it was outgoing artillery fire from the Paladins (155mm Howitzers) that night. They had been knocked to the ground by the blast wave from a rocket-assisted artillery round from a Paladin. In other words, they experienced a close encounter of the friendly-fire type.

Having close contact with several of the Iraqi people, Gray formed a positive opinion regarding them. "Ninety percent of them realized that we wanted to help them. They knew we were only going to be there long enough to do our jobs and then leave." The Iraqi soldiers oftentimes did not want to cause conflict with the Americans. "They didn't want to die; in fact, for the most part they didn't want to fight either." Gray did say, however, that those soldiers loyal to the old Saddam Hussein regime were known to be extremely cruel to Iraqi civilians. "We heard many stories of how they tortured their victims."

Gray said that he hopes that after American troops finally all return home, the Iraqi people can maintain their new-found freedom. "Many of those people didn't know what freedom was," says Gray, "especially the women and children." Gray also stated that while helping the Iraqis gain their freedom, he himself came to realize that Americans take their own freedom for granted. "We in America don't realize how few people in the world actually have freedom," he admits.

After one year and two days in Iraq, Gray and the rest of the 3664th MC finally began the long trip home. However, when he discovered that his time was up, he held bittersweet feelings. "I was happy, but I felt somewhat tempered because some units had just gotten their tours extended. Therefore, I didn't really celebrate out of respect." Because some units were having their tours extended, Gray says he was mindful that perhaps this could happen to his unit as well. "I wasn't really one hundred-percent sure I was coming home until I was halfway across the Atlantic. We had stopped in Germany to re-fuel, and I was still mindful we could turn around and go back."

However, after the stop in Germany, the 3664th reached its destination back at Fort Dix in the middle of the night. Once there, the company had to spend eight days before coming back to West Virginia. During that time, Gray and the others underwent several medical evaluations. "They had counselors, clergy, and psychiatrists on hand to help us adjust to being back. Plus, a lot of us were watching after each other." Gray said the biggest adjustment for him was getting re-accustomed to northeast February weather. "We went from very hot in the Iraqi desert to twenty-eight degrees at Fort Dix."

When the eight days expired, the 3664th MC flew into Charleston, West Virginia, to meet the families that they had not seen in over a year. Awaiting Gray in Charleston were his mother, Connie; sister, Diana; and others, including Braden. "I was in uniform and so tanned that Braden didn't recognize me at first," he laughed. "It took him a few moments." Gray's war experience was finally over.

Although Gray said that he has never suffered from any serious problems such as post-traumatic stress disorder, he admitted that adjusting back to life in the United States was somewhat difficult. "As weird as it sounds, it was hard to adapt to freedom and modern conveniences, like taking a shower any time I wanted. Plus, I missed the feeling of carrying a weapon. I had a 9mm pistol on me at all times in Iraq."

On September 30, 2005, at the age of forty-two, MSG Gray retired from the Active Army Reserves and West Virginia Army National Guard. However, he feels that it will always be a part of him. In fact, he believes that the military provided him with many wonderful experiences, and he would recommend it to young people today. Gray is surprisingly thankful for the opportunity to have served in Iraq. "It was the climax to my military career," he stated. Today, he works as a system accountant with the United States Treasury Department and Bureau of the Public Debt in Parkersburg, West Virginia. He enjoys spending time with Braden and reflects back with great pride that he served his country well.

About the author. Kaula Young is a resident of Letart, West Virginia. She is the daughter of Chastity and Niles Young. Kaula also has a younger sister, Haylee. She is a member of the Wahama High School softball team. In her spare time she likes hanging out with her friends and family. She also likes to just watch movies and listen to music. Upon graduation, she plans on attending West Virginia University to obtain a degree in dental hygiene.

Travis Gray's biggest apprehension about going to Iraq was leaving behind his young son, Braden.

David Hall

United States Army
Vietnam War

By Taylor Hysell

In 1967, eighteen-year-old David Hall of New Haven, West Virginia, found himself in the same place as many other young American men of the time—Vietnam; and like the rest of his countrymen, he served with honor and valor. Upon his return home, however, Hall found that his contributions to his fellow military brothers and sisters were not yet complete, for his journey through life after Vietnam has led him to years of service through the American Legion.

The Army drafted Hall shortly after his high school graduation. He remembers that his family did not handle the news of his draft very well. "We knew it was coming though," he recalls. Hall knew that some difficult situations awaited him, but he was going to do it for his country. He trained for twenty weeks at Fort Campbell, Kentucky, and Fort Dix, New Jersey, before he went to a place he knew very little about, which was Vietnam. Once arriving at his destination, he remembers it as being extremely hot. He was an infantry soldier stationed in Fut Vin. "The training was very good, but nothing could really prepare you for that," he recalls.

Hall described his living conditions as very poor. For instance, on most occasions he slept in open fields with no cover in extreme cold and wet circumstances. "Normally, I would get less than four hours of sleep at a time, and my body never got used to it. Through the daytime hours, it became extremely hot. And as for eating, the food was terrible," says Hall. "It was hard to get used to." Personal hygiene was at a minimum also, for many times Hall and his peers were deprived of opportunities for showers. "You couldn't really change clothes or shave very often either. Sometimes you may get to shower two or three times a week, and sometimes you might go two weeks without one. We weren't too pleasant to be around."

Being an infantry soldier, Hall saw an abundance of combat. Some of his daily routines consisted of boarding a helicopter or being on ambush patrol for one to ten days; then he would come back to his base for one or two days. Hall would take part in guard duty with four hours on and four hours off, and he would try to sleep for a few hours when he was off. The kind of equipment he was around consisted of items like armor, airplanes, helicopters and machine guns, but he only operated small arms as weapons.

There wasn't a large amount of free time when he was in the war, and even when there was a break, there wasn't much to do. They mostly sat around or caught up on their mail, which was the only way he could communicate with his family. "It took awhile for the letters to go back and forth," said Hall. He became good friends with his fellow soldiers and had a lot of respect for them. They kept in touch for several years following the war but eventually lost track of one another.

David Hall was a Staff Sergeant E-6 and felt like he had a purpose when he was fighting for his country. When he left Vietnam, the Army transferred him to Panama, where he served as a jungle warfare instructor, putting new soldiers through the same kind of training he had undergone. "We basically were getting people ready to go to Vietnam," he says.

Although the soldier wasn't treated well by the American people when he arrived home, he was still happy to be back safe and sound. "It certainly wasn't like it is now. I'm tickled to death the way it is right now," meaning the way that soldiers are being welcomed home on their returns from Iraq and Afghanistan. "At the time of Vietnam, everybody was kind of against the war, and they blamed the people that were in it. It would be nothing for people to spit on you in an airport. They just didn't handle it very well. I think that's part of the reason why the veterans of today are getting what they deserve, because a lot of them are the children of Vietnam veterans." Hall received the usual medals and was discharged in February 1970. Although he did consider remaining in the service, he eventually chose against it.

"It was hard getting used to normal life, because it was just different," says Hall. For instance, adapting to the change in temperatures provided quite a challenge. "When I got back home, I stayed cold for a very long time, mainly because everywhere I had been like Vietnam and Panama had been very, very hot. I remember coming home in February, and it was freezing cold. I didn't even have any winter clothes." Attempting to get his life back on track, he started working at West Virginia Malleable Iron in the town where he grew up, Point Pleasant. After he worked there a few years, he went to Sporn, Gavin, and then to Mountaineer, all power plants operated by American Electric Power Company. Hall still works there and has been employed by AEP for thirty-nine years.

David Hall was married to his wife Susan in 1990. He is a father of two and has four grandchildren. Family is a big part of his life, and he loves

Samuel Halstead

United States Army
World War II

By Randi Roush

"I remember we had three feet of snow once, and all I had to keep warm were the clothes I had on." Samuel Halstead of New Haven recalls all too well the winter of 1945. He spent most of it in a fox hole trying to stay alive. In addition to the harsh conditions and lack of supplies, Halstead also was attempting to survive the relentless artillery and gunfire from a desperate German army during one of World War II's most horrendous battles, the Battle of the Bulge.

Drafted at the young age of eighteen, Halstead served in one of the most devastating wars in history, World War II. Because of its magnitude, along with the fact that the United States military fought in both Europe and the Pacific, it surprised no young man at this time to receive a draft notice, and Halstead was no exception. In fact, as he turned old enough to become eligible in September 1943, he actually expected it, and it happened soon after. The draft took its toll on the Halstead family, as three of his brothers received draft letters as well, leaving his mom, brother, and three younger sisters behind. The youngest of the five brothers was given the opportunity to stay home in order to help their mother (whose husband had died just a few years earlier) and young sisters. Although Halstead anticipated military service with apprehension, he looked forward to serving his country.

Halstead left home and reported to Camp Blanding, located in north-central Florida, for basic training in January of 1944. There he spent thirteen weeks. He was to become part of the 36th Infantry Division. When asked if he thought the Army prepared him well to enter battle, he responded, "They did pretty well." Halstead recalls that his superiors in boot camp told him and the others that they were being trained specifically to fight the Germans. With the completion of basic training, his division headed across the Atlantic Ocean for Africa. In fact, the D-Day Invasion took place while Halstead was in route to Europe.

It didn't take long for Halstead to get placed in the heat of the action of World War II. While in route to Africa, his destination changed to Naples, Italy, where much action was taking place, such as air raids by the Germans and black-outs as defense tactics. Soon though, Halstead earned a promotion to sergeant and first scout and was sent to France (where he spent his nineteenth birthday) along the front lines during the Battle of the Bulge, one of the last major German offensives during the war. The Allied soldiers attempted, and eventually succeeded, to reach Germany and liberate it from the Nazis. "It was toward the end of the war," said Halstead, "and the Germans were on the run." Halstead recalled that many of the German soldiers by this time did not want to fight any longer and that some would even lay their weapons down and put their hands up. However, there were still enough willing Germans to put up more than a fair battle.

Halstead reflected on the type of fighting. "We had everything coming toward us. Artillery, mortar, tank fire—we had it all. Bombs came down from airplanes." After a while, his squad leader was wounded, so Halstead became the new one, which consisted of leading ten men. Most of the time, Halstead and his men fought in foxholes. "We didn't really have a routine; we just did what we could to survive," he stated. "I was scared lots of times."

Life in a foxhole was less than desirable. In fact, each one contained two soldiers who often spent several days and long nights alternating turns sleeping and keeping guard. Halstead recalled spending three months in foxholes fighting in the Battle of the Bulge during the winter months. "Of course, when there's that much snow, troops can't move as well. When I first went up to the front, I had a blanket, but on the first morning, we moved to take a hill, and I threw away everything but my ammunition and my rifle." To cover the foxholes and to serve as protection from the weather, the soldiers used branches, which unfortunately were often blown off by bombs. They had to always be alert, no matter what they were doing at the time. "We were in what they called the 'Defensive Position' because we were afraid the Germans were going to break through our lines."

Halstead vividly recalls one particular dicey situation he experienced when he served as a scout: "The job of the scout is to go out ahead and draw enemy fire. They [the Germans] had a machine gun set up and fired right above my head, hitting a limb right over me. You can bet I got out of that job right away. They didn't hit me, but I was lucky. After that, they made somebody else the scout."

Another time, Halstead remembers him and some others being ordered to sneak into the night and break the German lines in hopes of obtaining prisoners. "We came upon a big farm house. There was one German soldier standing there on guard. I yelled at him, and he ran. We rushed into the farm house and captured about fifty German soldiers. We took them back and questioned them. They were glad to actually be captured."

When asked what he and his friends did for entertainment, Halstead replied succinctly, "Kill Germans." He continued, "There really wasn't much to do for entertainment on the front lines. They only relieved you for about three or four days, and then you would take a shower, and after that, you'd go right back to the front lines." As for food on the front, Halstead said, "They had people cook for you sometimes, and then you had c-rations that you carried with you; sometimes you'd get a cooked meal, but not very often. It was really hard to eat out there in the field, but we got by."

On March 15, 1945, in the area around Strasburg, France, Sergeant Halstead received a gunshot wound to the chin while in his foxhole. "We were not too far from the Rhine River in the Haguenau Forest," he recalls. "I was behind a tree, and a sniper in a nearby tree to my right shot me through the jaw. It was getting close to where I live," Halstead laughed, pointing to his brain. "I was actually very lucky." This was the last combat that he ever saw, for he was quickly evacuated to receive medical attention. "We had medics right along with us, and just shortly after I was hit, a medic came along. He said 'You're not hurt too bad.' But the blood was flying everywhere, and after I found out that I wasn't hurt too badly, I thought to myself, 'This is a million-dollar wound—it's going to get me out of combat.' I was really fortunate that I wasn't really wounded too badly; in fact, it could have been a lot worse. Those German snipers—that's who shot me—usually hit their targets, but luckily this one shot low."

From the front lines, Halstead was transported to a field hospital, where his wounds were treated. Not long after, he then was moved to a more traditional hospital in France, followed by a transfer to another hospital in England, which is where Halstead was when the Germans surrendered. "There was a lot of celebrating," he said. Finally, another transfer ensued, this one to the United States. "I feel the doctors and the staffs at the hospitals did an excellent job," he says. Even today, Halstead still puts his faith in veterans' hospitals. Overall, he said he feels that the military does a very good job of taking care of its own.

When it came to keeping in touch with family, Halstead attempted to write letters to his mom every chance he could. "You didn't have a lot of time to write while in combat," he states. He received a letter about once a week, even though sometimes it was tough to get it when he was on the front lines. Although he never saw his three brothers while at war, he could write them. One day, he wrote to his oldest brother, James Norton Halstead, and sadly the letter was returned with the word "Deceased." This was how Halstead discovered that James had been killed while a member of the 82nd Airborne in France. Not only did Sam have to deal with being at war and away from his family, he couldn't dwell on his brother's loss as much as he wanted or needed. He had to forget about it and move on for the time being as a means of self-preservation.

On September 17, 1945, the hospital discharged him, and the Army did likewise on the same day. For his heroics on the battlefield, Halstead received several medals, among them the Purple Heart and the Bronze Star. "One of the top generals, George C. Marshall, had said that all soldiers who received a Combat Infantry Badge would receive the Bronze Star medal. The basis for doing this was that those soldiers had borne the hardships of battle." Despite the hardships, the trauma, and the wound, Halstead says that overall, the military provided him with a valuable experience. "I was glad to have gone and served my country. It was my responsibility."

Shortly after returning home in 1945, he recalls having some nightmares. His wife, Helen, stated, "When I first met him, he was really depressed. He had just come home from the war, and he was down in the dumps. But I don't think it lasted too long."

Today, at age eighty-three, Halstead still gets along very well and remains as active as possible. He and Helen have been married for sixty-two years and have three sons—Ed (who served four years in the U.S. Navy during the Vietnam War), Tim, and Steve—and have seven grandchildren and five great-grandchildren. Tim summed up his father's war experience this way: "I was always proud of him, but for years he never talked about the war. Now that I know about his experience, I'm proud because he is part of the greatest generation that ever lived."

About the author. Randi Roush and her family are residents of Letart, West Virginia. She is the daughter of Eddie and Lisa Roush and enjoys riding horses with her family in the summer. In school, she is a member of the color guard in the Wahama Marching Band. Randi is also a member of the National Honor Society. For fun, she enjoys hanging out with friends, watching movies, listening to music, and going to the mall. After high school, Randi plans to attend college to earn a degree in the medical field.

As a member of the 36th Infantry Division in France, Samuel Halstead was wounded in the Battle of the Bulge. Here he poses alongside his Purple Heart.

John Hayman

United States Marine Corps
World War II

By Kierstan White

Growing up in Leon, West Virginia, in the 1930's, John Hayman probably dreamed of adventures in faraway places. Those places, however, likely never included the Pacific island of Saipan. It was this island, though, that served as the setting for Hayman's most terrifying memories as a Marine during World War II.

Hayman never expected to get drafted at the age of nineteen, but that is exactly what happened. He was chosen to serve in the United States Marine Corps, which promptly whisked him off to Parris Island for twelve weeks of basic training. "As soon as I got there, I was stripped of my civilian clothes and went through what they called a 'de-louser,' where they showered you down and sprayed you. Then they threw a poncho at you," said Hayman. Soon afterward, he and the other new Marines were provided military clothing. He recalls that it took them about a week to become completely settled. Hayman's instructors soon placed him and the others in a platoon.

"The first thing we learned," commented Hayman, "was 'you're here, you have a drill instructor, and he does all your thinking for you. I'm your mommy, and I'm your daddy now.'" The instructors attempted to instill in their young students an ability to survive amidst the hardships they would encounter in combat during World War II. "Basic training was to merely teach us how to basically take care of ourselves, take care of our clothes. They issued you a certain amount of clothing—socks and boots, for example—and that was your job, to take care of that stuff," he continued.

According to Hayman, he and his fellow Marines were well taken care of. "We were in need of nothing," he said. "Every morning they would have a sick call, and if you had a blister or anything like that, they took care of it. Yet at the same time they instilled in us survival." According to Hayman, one method the instructors used for teaching survival skills to the young Marines was to develop a general dislike for humanity.

After basic training, Hayman's next stop was Camp Lejeune, North Carolina. This Marine base provided Hayman with his final stages of training before his dispatch overseas. Next, the men traveled by bus to Norfolk, Virginia, where they boarded a ship headed to the Pacific. Their route took them down the East coast and along the Atlantic Ocean until they reached the Panama Canal. From there, they sailed to Pearl Harbor.

Upon arriving at Pearl Harbor, the Marines assigned each man a new unit, receiving additional training. After this, even more training was attained on the Hawaiian island of Maui for about six additional weeks. "We were busy every single day," said Hayman. "They barely gave you time to write a letter home, and that's about it. They kept you moving and didn't give you time to think, only what they wanted you to think. There was certainly no time to get homesick either."

Hayman's training aptly prepared him for battle, and he found that out when the Marines assigned him to a unit that fought on the island of Saipan. Hayman remembers being loaded into an amtrack and being unable to see the enemy until the doors of the watercraft had come down. The Marines then waded onto shore, evading bullets and mortars all the while. Hayman recalls seeing many wounded Marines as he charged onto the beach of the small island.

Once on the island, Hayman remembered what his boot camp instructors taught him. "The main thing was survival," he said. "All you had to cling to was hope." Hayman spoke of a young man he remembered from his platoon who had fought in combat before Saipan who read his New Testament during every free moment. "He knew this was going to be his last battle," recalled Hayman with teary eyes, "and indeed, he did not make it. If a bullet is meant for you, it will find you."

Hayman admits that at his age during the Battle of Saipan, he was oblivious to the possibility of death. "I just didn't think about it. This was what I was supposed to do, and I did it," he said. However, although a bullet never found Hayman, a mortar did. As soon as it landed and exploded near him, Hayman was blown right out of his boots, knocking him several feet from where he stood. "I had on a brand new pair of Marine Corps shoes," he said. Shrapnel from the mortar flew into his right hand in between two fingers, but the most painful wound was from the shrapnel that lodged inside his leg. Although Hayman remembers it burning like fire, he never lost consciousness. When asked if he saw and heard the mortar coming, he replied emphatically, "Oh yeah. Things were just flying everywhere."

After being wounded, medics arrived almost immediately, loaded him up, and transported him via an amtrack to a hospital ship that specialized in treating the injured. "The amtracks were constantly going back and forth," he said. They carried in fresh soldiers and supplies and transported the wounded to the hospital ship. Hayman remained on the hospital ship, receiving treatment for his wounds, while the battle continued. He recalls getting several shots of morphine for the intense pain resulting from the shrapnel. These shots went on for about two weeks.

His next stop featured a return visit to Pearl Harbor, where he recovered for approximately six weeks. Following this, he was transferred to a Naval hospital just outside of Oakland, California. Finally, Hayman received surgery for his wounds in Long Island, New York. While there, the military awarded him the Purple Heart. After recovery, he was dispatched back to Camp Lejeune, where he was in a redistribution battalion. "What we mainly did was go around and pick up cigarette butts and other trash. They always found something there for you to do."

As he prepared to return to California, Hayman recalls being on guard duty when he heard an announcement about the dropping of the first atom bomb. "It wasn't soon after that they sent us all home," he recalled. Hayman remembers getting a "ruptured duck"—a small bird-shaped medal—upon his discharge in 1945, to wear on his uniform.

Despite the horrors of battle, Hayman's feelings toward his military years are mostly good ones. "I loved the service," he explained. "It did a lot for me. The Marines treated us very well. I really have no complaints. I just did what needed to be done. I have no regrets."

Throughout his time in the Marines, Hayman says that people, both military and civilian, treated him very kindly and with respect. "In every hospital I was in while recovering from my wounds, the civilians treated me first-class," he said. "You could be walking down the street on a Saturday afternoon, and someone might pull up and invite you to dinner. The uniform really meant something to people in that day."

Once home, Hayman remembers experiencing many difficulties. One, surprisingly enough, was having so much free time. Hayman mentioned that while in the Marine Corps, he became so accustomed to his superiors telling him what to do that having choices made for quite an adjustment. Hayman also recalls difficulty in finding a job. "You couldn't even get an application," he said. "I finally went to the agent on the New York Central Railroad in Leon and asked if I could sit with him and learn to be a telegraph operator." This led to a railroad job in Indiana making sixty cents an hour. "If you worked the night shift, they gave you an extra dime." It was while working for the railroad that Hayman met the woman who has now been his wife for sixty-two years. Together, they have four daughters, one of which followed her father into the military. The couple also boasts of several children and grandchildren. Now eighty-five, Hayman remains extremely humble in regards to his heroics sixty-five years ago on a tiny island that proved instrumental to the Allied campaign against the Japanese during World War II.

About the Author. Kierstan White, born on February 26, 1992, is a current resident of New Haven, West Virginia, and attends Wahama High School. She is the daughter of Franklin and Jennifer White and comes from a large family. She enjoys spending time with her family and friends during her free time. After high school she plans to attend college and go into the medical field.

John Hayman fought in the Battle of Saipan during World War II. Here he is shown with student-author Kierstan White.

Golden Herdman

United States Army National Guard
Operation Iraqi Freedom

By Miriam Gordon

Although brave and distinguished, Golden Herdman of Point Pleasant could not really be considered your typical soldier. During the prime of his life, the Vietnam War took place, and as a member of the National Guard, he fortunately was never chosen to participate. However, as the new millennium began, another war broke out, this time in Iraq. Now in his fifties, this chief warrant officer received the call to serve his country overseas in what would be characterized as a hostile war environment.

Golden Herdman was the chief warrant officer over the electronics repair section for the 3664th Maintenance Company. Proud of his title, he proved to be very deserving of each rank that he was presented. During his life, he spent thirty-nine years and seven months in the National Guard. He says, "I'm glad that I had the chance to help out. It's hard for individuals to realize what a solider goes through and does. I'm just happy to have gone and come back safe."

In 1966, this then-nineteen-year-old went with his friend to take the test to join the National Guard. The test helped decide the kinds of jobs each new enlistee would be best qualified to perform. Obviously, the higher the score, the more options a person had. Herdman did especially well on the electronics part of the test, enabling him to obtain training in the field of electronic repair. After signing up, boot camp became the next priority. He partook in this rigorous preparatory instruction at Fort Knox, Kentucky. "The first thing I had to do was get the GI hair cut," he says. Next, the Guard put Herdman through some of the hardest training that he had ever experienced. Marching, lack of sleep, and physical training eventually became an everyday experience. "We spent a lot of time on the rifle range. Everyone had to qualify in the use of a rifle." While receiving this weapons training, he also learned how to kill the enemy no matter what, whether with a gun, knife, hands, or anything else available. He spent many a night with another person

Golden Herdman gets interviewed for this project by student-author
Miriam Gordon.

Roger Hughart

United States Army
Vietnam War

By Brandon Johnson

In 1966 in between college stints, the unexpected happened to Roger Hughart: he received a draft notice. At just 20 years of age, Hughart was told to report to Army training in just three short weeks, barely enough time to say good-bye and prepare for what was probably going to be the biggest challenge of his life. Within a few months Hughart found himself on a plane as an Army private heading toward the dangerous war in Vietnam. Approximately three weeks into his tour, however, Hughart felt elation to discover that he had been transferred out of the volatile country to what he thought was a safer place: Korea. Hughart soon found out though that Korea still provided some violent situations of its own.

Hughart served in the Infantry Division in both Korea and Vietnam. "I felt safer in Korea, but I was still scared and fearful that I might get hurt or killed," he states. Even though Hughart was an operations and communications specialist, or sometimes called an E-4 Specialist, the war was still very scary. As an E-4 Specialist, Hughart maintained and repaired any and all of the radio and communications equipment used. As an operator he kept in touch with the front lines, battalions, aid stations, and other sites and divisions that needed to keep in contact with others. Even though they were in a dangerous war, the equipment was good and well maintained, considering the conditions in which it was used.

"The conditions in Korea were good for being in a violent area," says Hughart. "We slept in Army-issue bunk beds, in a fairly safe and secure place, and ate decent food." Hughart survived each day by keeping a large calendar on the wall, and after seeing each day pass, he crossed it off. His quest for survival was further enhanced by his superiors, who were short on compassion; in fact, they possessed none.

Although the Demilitarized Zone is a no-firing zone, there are a few shootings that occasionally occur. Today, it is the most heavily militarized border in the world, at a staggering 155 miles long and 2.5 miles wide. Even though he was stationed at the Demilitarized Zone, or DMZ, one incident occurred that threatened his life. In the middle of the night, Hughart patrolled on guard duty, under the only light around the hillside. All of a sudden, he heard two shots ring out from the other side of the zone. Not knowing what to do, his human instinct kicked in, and he dove on his stomach away from the flying bullets. Hearing the bullets whistle as they flew by, Hughart prayed that he would not get shot. After yelling for help, he did not move until two or three of his fellow soldiers arrived to back him up and safely get him off the hillside. "It felt like an eternity," says Hughart, "but I was never so glad to see my buddies come running up that hill to rescue me." He thought that this might get some compassion from his commanders, but they just ignored it. Hughart never dreamed that he would get shot at more in Korea than in Vietnam, especially at the DMZ, where a person can almost stand on one side of the fence and stare into the eyes of a North Korean. He added that in all of the other patrols in which he partook, he was a lot more cautious and careful than the time before. Even with this being the most secured border in the world in 1968, which was during Hughart's tour, thirty-one North Koreans disguised as South Koreans crossed the border. Their objective was to assassinate South Korean President Park Chung Hee. Fortunately, the mission failed, the North Koreans were defeated, and Hee was never harmed.

As each day passed, Hughart knew that it would not be long until he returned home and escaped the violence of Southeast Asia. Like most other soldiers, he greatly anticipated seeing his family and friends once again. However, one day he and his buddies received some very bad news: their tours of duty had been extended another thirty days. "After we all got the news, we were scared that all of us may not get to go home," responded Hughart.

However, after getting through those extra thirty days, an excited Hughart heard his orders to return home. Anxiously awaiting a joyful appearance back in the United States amid congratulatory handshakes and pats on the back for serving his country, he unfortunately found the opposite. Thousands of Americans showed their hatred and resentment toward the Vietnam War by taking it out on those who fought in it. Hughart remembers protesters shouting "baby killers" and spitting on the Vietnam veterans at airports when they returned home. "Even some of the soldiers would get beaten and hit as they walked along the streets and airports," Hughart recalls. Despite these mean-spirited acts of violence toward the heroic men who fought in battle, Hughart maintains pride in both the efforts of him and his country. "I'm happy to have served in the Army and to have helped preserve the country's freedom," he says. Although he may not have gotten any medals for serving in the military, the memories of all his buddies that fought with him, he says, is all that he needs.

Unfortunately, despite finally being home, Hughart's experiences in both Vietnam and Korea lived on in painful memories and dreams. Like many veterans of this era, he faced some of the worst nightmares that he has ever experienced. "Each night for eight years, I would wake up having a nightmare about an experience that happened in Vietnam or Korea. Even still today I have one every now and then, and will for the rest of my life."

In spite of the all the bad experiences and painful memories, Hughart, like most war veterans, would do it all again if called upon. In fact, he says he would be interested in returning to Vietnam today. "I'd like to see how the people, towns, and beautiful landscapes have changed over the years." However, he admits, "Even if I wanted to go back and fight, they would not let me." Probably one of the reasons why would be because Hughart in recent years has suffered from several health issues, most notably throat cancer, which has limited his ability to speak.

When Hughart returned home from the war, he began to live a normal civilian life. After working in local industrial plants for about nine years, he decided to return to college to fulfill his desire to attain a good education, which is what he had been doing before he received his draft notice. Upon completing his degree requirements, Hughart began teaching special education at Wahama High School, where he remains today.

About the Author: Brandon Johnson grew up in the rural community of Letart, West Virginia, on a small beef cattle farm. He is the only child of Larry and Lisa Johnson and is a senior at Wahama High School in Mason, West Virginia. He enjoys riding four-wheelers, playing golf, hunting, fishing, and hanging out with his friends. He also hopes to go to college and get a degree in electrical engineering at WVU Tech.

Roger Hughart experienced an unusual incident by getting transferred from Vietnam to Korea.

Paul Johnson

United States Army
Vietnam Veteran

By Kylee Henry

Roughly 2.7 million Americans served in uniform in Vietnam in the 1960's and '70's. However, in addition to the fracas transpiring in Southeast Asia, the Cold War proceeded in other parts of the world as well. For this reason, the American service men and women of this era were dispatched to many other sites throughout the country and the world to insure our nation's safety from the dangers of the Soviet Union and its Communist allies. One such soldier who protected our borders in a different way other than fighting in Vietnam was Paul Johnson of Mason.

Johnson was only twenty years old when he enlisted into the United States Army. He spent three years in the military while achieving his highest rank as Specialist 4. Like many of his peers in the 1960's-70's era, he enlisted into the service, mainly because he knew he would eventually be drafted. In addition, he also felt a sense of duty to his country. During this era of American history, all men registered for the draft at the age of eighteen. "They went down a list of birthdays, and when they came to yours, if you had not already enlisted, they picked something for you," Johnson explained. According to Johnson, one advantage to enlisting during this time was that one was privileged to pick his job and destination. Johnson recalls being given a list of jobs to choose from at the time of his enlistment. "At least this way, you got to choose your own destiny," he stated. "If you were drafted, they lined you up at the reception center and told you whether you were going in the Army, Navy, or Marines." Hence, young men were given little if any choice as to their preferred station and usually were dispatched to Vietnam.

Like all new soldiers, Johnson's first stop along his military journey was basic training. Afterward, he furthered his skills at Fort Bliss, Texas, for what he termed advanced individual training, or AIT. Army personnel at Fort Bliss prepared Johnson for his MOS (military occupation specialty) in the Army Air Defense, an Army artillery branch that specializes in anti-aircraft weapons. From here it was on to the Army Air Defense's Missile Systems, which he enjoyed very much, mainly because this unit stationed him in the area near Miami, Florida, home to a Florida Everglades missile site. "Missiles were placed there after the Cuban Missile Crisis around 1962," said Johnson. "They put them there for the protection of the Southern part of the United States."

This site became known as the Nike Hercules Missile Base HM-69. Nike Hercules missiles had a range of 110 miles, leaving them a bit short of striking Cuba, which was 160 miles away. Instead, the Army used them to block prospective incoming attacks. At the height of the Cold War, anti-aircraft missiles stood at the ready in Florida's swamplands, protecting the South from a potential Soviet nuclear bomber attack launched from Cuba.

Johnson's main duty consisted of working as a fire control crewman. "I was on a crew that operated radars that tracked the objects. For instance, if the object was an incoming airplane, then it would get taken out of the air," he stated. His daily routine consisted of equipment checks, clean-ups, and training. "We trained almost every day," said Johnson. "There was a lot of technical training. You had to learn to operate radars." For one of his training exercises, airplanes flew that dropped aluminum balls in order to see if the radars would pick them up. "That's what the enemies would do. You would have to learn to keep the target on the plane and not drop off on what was coming out of the plane. We would train on this about every month." In addition, Johnson was also expected to pull his share of guard duty at the site. "We had a secret security clearance, meaning that what we were working on wasn't top secret, but secret."

One of Johnson's most vivid memories consisted of a missile launch that he witnessed. "We had the opportunity to go to White Sands Missile Range in New Mexico, and we actually fired a missile." He continued, "Even though it was only for practice, it was very interesting. Plus, in the process I got to meet a lot of different people from many different places." There he and his peers helped set up the equipment for the launch. After they fired the missiles at the target, they would score it to test its accuracy. These records proved very vital for future reference in regard to other missile launches.

Another of Johnson's more vivid remembrances included what he termed "pulling surveillance" for Richard Nixon when he visited Key Biscayne, Florida, the location of one of the former-President's summer homes. "We would have to sit and watch the radars between us and Cuba," he said. "That was really a pretty boring job, but I did get to shake his hand one time right before he boarded Air Force One." Johnson recalls this occurring just a few months before Nixon's impeachment.

During free time, Johnson remembers himself having it pretty easy. "While being in South Florida, there are plenty of things to do. We spent most of the time at the beach." A funny thing he recalls is when he and his friends would catch rattlesnakes and turn them loose on the site to play with them and tease the other men. Being stateside, Johnson's living conditions were different than those of the men overseas—he lived off-site in an Army base housing facility. He said the food wasn't too good at basic training, somewhat the same as school food, but it got a lot better after he completed training. To keep in touch with his family, Johnson would write letters and talk to them on the telephone. Again, being stateside had its advantages.

When released from duty, Johnson said the process was simple: "You basically gave them your papers, and they paid for your expenses back home and to get your life started again."

Johnson recalls that upon his discharge, the security of the nation impressed him. "There were missile sites all over the country, not just in Florida. Most people have no idea where they are. They could be very close to them, and they wouldn't know," he said. As for the recent terror attacks in 2001, Johnson says that perhaps the nation's security advisors became just a little lax thinking that nothing like that would ever happen to this country.

Johnson feels very confident that the military helped to prepare him for his career and life after his discharge. "It just overall helped in my daily life," he said proudly. "It broadens your horizon in everything that you do—just what you do and what you see. It was just a great experience; in fact, everyone should experience the military—not war, but the military in general. It offers tremendous opportunities in terms of training." He said his military experience influenced his thought on wars. "When you're in the military, you really get a good idea of why you are there and why they are necessary. It's different than reading it out of a book."

Today, Johnson works at Alcan Rolled Products in Ravenswood, West Virginia. He also volunteers much of his time with the fire department in his hometown. Johnson feels that the military experience that he gained has aided him greatly in his career and with his voluntary job with the fire department. He and his wife, Karen, reside in Mason, West Virginia.

Like all of the other military men who served stateside during wartime, Paul Johnson felt extremely fortunate. Yet, like the others, he says that he would have proudly gone to Vietnam if needed. Although his services were not required overseas, Johnson served in an important capacity of another kind—helping to protect our nation's borders. When asked about his overall impression about his military experience, he humbly replies, "I was just glad to have served my country."

About the Author. Kylee Henry of Mason, West Virginia, is the daughter of Jeff Henry and Emily Henry. She is the older sister of twins Hope and Faith. As a senior at Wahama High School, Kylee has been involved in the flag corps and cheerleading.

Paul Johnson spent much of his time in the Army operating radars at the Nike Hercules Missile Base HM-69 in the Florida Everglades.

Don Justis

United States Marine Corps
Korean and Vietnam Wars

By Micaiah Branch

The uniform is old—probably almost forty years—yet it still fits seventy-four year-old Marine Don Justis as if it were new. He has adorned it once again for a special occasion, and he certainly stands out among the crowd. Perhaps it is because of the handsome white hair on top of his head, or maybe it's the abundance of medals pinned to his left breast; or it might just be the uniform itself, for it shows the spirit and pride that have come to symbolize the man who fought for his country in two wars.

At the young age of seventeen, Don Justis enlisted in the Marine Corps to serve his country. "I had always had my heart set on joining the Marines," he says. A rigorous and challenging boot camp followed. Justis knew that it would not be easy, but all too soon he found the difficulty was beyond his imagination. "The first thing you do is get off the bus, and then you run, and you don't stop running until you get back on the bus. I've been in two wars, and boot camp was worse," Justis laughs. "Marine Corps boot camp is rough—as rough as I've had it." If a Marine messed up during marching, he got hit in the foot with the butt of his own rifle. Getting caught with cigarettes meant the entire pack would be placed in the mouth of the guilty Marine and lit at once, all while having a bucket over his head.

Just two weeks before being shipped to Korea, Justis married his sweetheart. It was tough leaving his bride, but he said he had an obligation to serve, no matter who or what he had to leave at home. He explains, "I went where they told me to go. I didn't ask questions."

In Korea, Justis served as a machine gunner in a rifle company attached to a weapons platoon consisting of thirty men, in which he was the platoon leader. When a field, city, or hill needed to be taken, Justis and his fellow Marines were called into action. "I was a line company Marine," he says. "In combat, a Marine is always out front. This included patrols, ambushes, and night patrols." The main goal during a routine patrol was to find and eliminate the enemy. "It was search and destroy. Your squadron searched out the area, you found the enemy, and you tried to destroy him. Sometimes you succeed, and sometimes you don't, and that's just the way it goes." These patrols sometimes lasted up to a week. After Justis's squad located the enemy, they either called in for artillery or for an air strike. On quite a few occasions, Justis recalls locating the enemy by being fired upon first. Luckily for him, enemy fire never struck him, although several of his men were hit. In fact, Justis remembers losing many men to combat, although he is unsure of the death toll. "Once we came in and did our job, we left as others came in to sweep the area. They were accountable for recovering the bodies of the dead." He also remembers being in some dangerous situations where he and his men evaded bombs and rockets.

Justis remembers that there were distinct differences between the Korean landscape and that of the United States. The terrain consisted of many rugged hills, and the temperatures in the winter often dropped as low as minus-twenty-four degrees. Although the weather provided quite a challenge, Justis modestly states that he somehow grew accustomed to it.

After his tour in Korea ended, the Marine returned home, but civilian life proved difficult. Although the war changed him tremendously, he moved on with his life with his bride. Justis, however, had decided to make a career of the military, and a little over a decade later, another conflict led him back to combat. Justis admits that he knew very little about Vietnam at the time, although it did not take long to learn about it, for in 1966 he discovered the war-torn nation on a personal level. "Korea and Vietnam were nothing alike. They were like day and night. Korea was very cold. Vietnam was warm with a lot of monsoons. Whereas in Korea you had mountains, in Vietnam there were jungles."

This time as he departed for war, in addition to leaving behind a wife, Justis had to say goodbye to a son. "It was hard to leave my family behind but once I got over there, I didn't think about anything else but fighting the enemy. I had to in order to survive."

Justis remembers that the majority of the South Vietnamese people welcomed the Marines and appreciated their efforts. "We interacted with the men and women and children, as long as the North Vietnamese weren't around," he says.

During one of their routine patrol missions, Justis's company drew enemy fire while crossing an open area. Immediately, Justis and his men hit the ground, going into an escape procedure known as the leap frog. The men made a straight line from the ground, and the man at the end of the line would run to the front about twenty-five yards ahead of the others. This maneuver continued until the enemy fire ceased. This time, however, the

North Vietnamese resumed firing. The leap frog had not succeeded. Justis then called in the artillery, and he and his men began the leap frog process once again. After the firing failed to stop, he then called in an air strike, but the enemy did not give up their offensive. Following a period of continuous shooting, the North Vietnamese soldiers became confused and ran. As a result of his bravery and decision-making in a time of extreme crisis, Justis received the Silver Star, the third-highest honor a member of the military can receive. To acquire a Silver Star, one must show extreme bravery. As a result of Justis's quick response to a dangerous situation, only two men died with three being wounded. Justis's actions prevented additional casualties.

When asked to reflect upon his return home from Vietnam, Justis replied with a single word: "Bad." On their trip home, his commander told him and the others not to retaliate after anything. As they departed their plane, people yelled, spit, and cursed at them. Soldiers that had done nothing but follow orders were ridiculed and called indescribable names. "People will still do that kind of thing today. It happened to me not too long ago at a store," he says.

Once again, Justis was forced to adapt to civilian life. "You get used to war. For the longest time, I just couldn't cope with being a civilian." Justis returned from Vietnam with a much different perspective on life. Even today, flashbacks about battles and nightmares about lost friends haunt him. Many memories are too traumatic to think or speak about. "It's called post-traumatic stress disorder," says Justis, "and many men and women coming back from war have it. It usually just hits you all at once." Sometimes Justis relieves the panic that he feels just by walking away and being by himself.

Even though Justis luckily escaped both Korea and Vietnam without any injuries, he fears the effects that Agent Orange may have had on him. This was the code name for a chemical used by the military to clear the dense jungles in an effort to keep the enemy from hiding in them. In recent decades, the military and U.S. government have been highly criticized for this herbicide's use in Vietnam. "At the time the troops didn't know much, if anything, about it. Today it's causing cancer and all kinds of trouble for the men who were over there." Justis says that he is certain that he was exposed to this agent on several occasions.

On the day of his discharge, Justis said that he ironically felt no relief. "I wanted to stay [in the military], but because my family was tired of traveling, they wanted me to retire." After a twenty-year career in the Marine Corps, Justis did just that—he retired and returned to Mason County, where he became a coal miner. Today Justis still has not completely given up the life of a Marine. He volunteers at the V.A. hospital in Huntington, West Virginia, where he helps veterans that have been disabled from fighting in wars. He performs many tasks for these men. For instance, he pushes them in their wheel chairs, helps them walk, or takes them outside if they just need to smoke. At home, he loves riding horses, and even occasionally attends rodeos. Today, as he wears the Marine Corps signature dress blue uniform, he exemplifies the slogan, "Once a Marine, always a Marine."

About the Author. Micaiah Branch was born on March 9th, 1992, the fifth boy out of six. Currently, he is a senior at Wahama High School in Mason, West Virginia. He is actively involved in football and wrestling, and is in a power lifting club run by his dad. Micaiah plans to go on to college someday and enter the medical field to become an athletic physician.

Gunnery Sergeant Don Justis poses in front of a machine gun that his platoon seized in Operation Mameluke Thrust on June 11, 1968.

Brian Kearns

United States Army
Vietnam War

By Colin Pierce

Brian Kearns speaks gruffly and loudly, although it does not take long to see his soft side. For instance, talk to this long-time Mason, West Virginia, resident about any subject, and sooner or later he will give you a hearty laugh. His happy-go-lucky mood, however, hides the memories of nearly forty years ago—the ones, in fact, that he would rather forget but cannot.

Before the Vietnam War, Kearns, then twenty-one, lived in a simple upstairs apartment in Toledo, Ohio. He supported his wife, Sharon, and himself by working for the railroad as a teletype operator, but he soon changed his occupation, working at the General Motors plant helping to build transmissions. One day when the mail arrived, bad news came with it. "My landlady lived downstairs, and Sharon and I lived upstairs. She always put my mail on the banister, and the letter on the top of it was the draft paper. When I looked out the door and saw that down there, I told Sharon, '*You* go down there and get the mail.'" Kearns admits, however, that the letter really came as no surprise. Thousands of young men were being drafted, and in his case, it was a matter of *when* instead of *if*.

Kearns recalls that after he received his notice, he had ten days to report. However, with three days remaining before his deadline, he went to Point Pleasant and enlisted for three years instead. Enlistment held many advantages. "This way I could have a little more choice in what I was to do. They gave me a test, and it showed I was most qualified to be a crew chief—for the mechanical part of helicopters." In addition, enlistment gave him ten extra days with Sharon.

Even though his mother was not exactly thrilled by her son's enlistment, Kearns' father, who had served in World War II, took the news a little easier. Sharon, however, described herself as a wreck. "We'd only been married nine months when the draft notice came," she says, "and then a couple of months later, I found out I was pregnant." Before Kearns left, he moved Sharon back home to Mason.

Basic training in Fort Knox, Kentucky, gave Kearns an eye-opening experience to the war that he would soon enter. "Basic training was mostly physical," says Kearns. "It involved a lot of running, walking, hiking and training on different things like people shooting over your head. We also camped out in different places." After basic training, Kearns began his classes as a helicopter crew chief. "They told us all about the helicopter, from top to bottom, from front to back. Everything there was to know about that helicopter, we had to know it—the hydraulic systems of it, the mechanical part of it, how it flies, how to work on it, and all that kind of stuff."

After almost two years in the Army receiving various forms of training, Kearns finally was sent to Vietnam. He remembers his first stop being the city of Danang. There, he was loaded into a Chinook, a two-bladed helicopter that served to transport large numbers of troops, and taken to Camp Evans for a week of training. While at Camp Evans, Kearns was trained by North Vietnamese soldiers who had surrendered and agreed to show the Americans the tactics of the Vietcong. Kearns remembers, "These guys would be in their camouflage, and they would be telling us stuff, and the next thing you knew, one would have you by the foot. You didn't even know they were there. That's just how slick they could come up to you."

Kearns' job in Vietnam was a machine gunner on a Huey helicopter. "There were two gunners on a helicopter, one on each side. I was on the left. We had M-16's, an M-60 machine gun, and an M-79 grenade launcher. We didn't have to use the grenade launcher too much though. It was a single-shot just like a shotgun. Mostly we used it for phosphorus rounds, which would burn the surrounding area."

As a result of this duty, Kearns saw quite a bit of combat, most of it around Khe Sanh, Laos, and, as he says, "just about everywhere I went over there. I was all over the northern part of South Vietnam, including the DMZ." His daily routine consisted of flying on missions to transport troops in order to get them to various combat areas. "We dropped off men so they could get in there and secure a place. Then we'd set up base there and then fly back out. Then we'd supply food and ammunition to the guys on the ground. We'd also fly to places where they couldn't get to in jeeps. We might have to land our helicopter in some rough places as much as five or six times a day. It just depended on how many helicopters were taking part in the mission. On one mission we had one hundred and thirteen helicopters going in, and each helicopter could transport five men. So on that mission we only had to land once in that hostile area."

Kearns remembers landing several times as his helicopter received heavy enemy fire. "Basically when we took in troops to take over a place, there was a lot of fire and a lot of fire power. The jet planes—the F-4's—would go through and bomb the enemy, and then we would fly in and get shot at. Then we'd land and drop the guys off, and then back up we'd go." According to Kearns, after countless times of performing this same routine, he never quite got used to it. "The life expectancy of a crew chief or machine gunner was about thirty seconds after you hit the ground, so it was always in my mind, 'Am I going to make it back today?'"

Kearns' base was called Camp Eagle. It was usually about a forty-five-minute flight from there to the location of the combat. One day at Camp Eagle, Kearns received some fantastic news—his tour was over. After serving in Vietnam for twelve months, Kearns finally received notice that he was being sent home. "Actually, to be exact, it was eleven months and fourteen days," he laughed. Not only was his Vietnam tour ending, but so was his three-year term in the Army.

Even after his discharge in December 1971, the side effects remained. "When he came back home," says Sharon, "he wasn't really any different. Then after a while as he aged, things began to change." For instance, nightmares began. In addition, Kearns feels that the Agent Orange used during the Vietnam War has led to problems, such as his diabetes. "The Agent Orange was really potent," says Kearns. "It killed trees and everything in its path." Veterans oftentimes say that sometimes little things back home will remind them of experiences from the war, but that isn't so for Kearns, except for one thing: helicopters. "Today when I hear a helicopter flying overhead, I'll go outside and look at it. It's just something that gets in your blood, I guess."

When Kearns returned home, not only was Sharon waiting on him, but his two-year-old daughter, Sonia, who had been born before he had shipped off to Vietnam. "I got to be with her during her first year, but I was in Vietnam when she started to walk and talk," he said.

"Everything got back to normal after about a year," Kearns continued in regard to civilian life after his three-year Army stint. "In Vietnam, you had to worry about not seeing your family, whether you were going to make it back or not—all of a sudden it was lifted off your shoulders—when you got back, you were more or less free. I wasn't free over there."

Looking back, Kearns says flat-out, "I didn't like the war—period. That country was so far back in time in 1971 that it was pathetic. I mean, they lived in straw houses, and everything around them was terrible. What we were even fighting for, I couldn't tell you. They wanted to keep them free from Communism, but the Vietnamese really didn't have any freedom."

Although to this day he fails to understand the rationale behind the war, he is still proud that he had the opportunity to serve his country.

Today, Brian Kearns is a well-respected and well-known citizen of Mason, where he has lived just about his entire civilian life. He and Sharon are the proud parents of two daughters (Sonia and Amber), one son (B.W.), and several grandchildren. After working for several years after his discharge, he is now happily retired. If you see Kearns about town, he'll greet you with his trademark smile and a quick wisecrack, and it's easy to tell that he enjoys his life. Thank goodness the scars that remain from a war four decades ago haven't ruined his outlook for the future.

About the Author. Colin Pierce is the son of Randy and Beth Pierce and brother of Nolan Pierce. A senior at Wahama High School, he participates in varsity football and choir. Most importantly, he is an honor student with high hopes and expectations for a lucrative career, most likely in a sports- or science-related field.

Vietnam veteran Brian Kearns held the position of machine gunner on a Huey helicopter.

Edward Kincaid

United States Navy
Vietnam War

By Scott Scarberry

Eddie Kincaid bounces into a room with the energy of a playful dog. His sociable, humorous demeanor seems contagious when around him for just a short period of time. A positive disposition of this manner likely provided a tremendous aid for the Point Pleasant resident during his time in Vietnam in the 1960's. In fact, it may have contributed greatly to his decision to re-enlist just so he could be sent to Vietnam and help out in the war-torn country.

Born on May 5, 1943, Kincaid enjoyed a normal youth and graduated from Point Pleasant High School. After graduation, however, he was like a lot of other teenagers who really didn't quite yet have a direction for his life. He felt he wasn't really college material, so with few other options available, he enlisted in the Navy in June 1960. "I really didn't want to do much of anything," he says, "but get out of Point Pleasant, so I joined the Navy." After completing a four-year term of naval service in April 1964, Kincaid re-enlisted in 1966 for an additional two years. Almost immediately afterward, the Navy sent him to Vietnam. "Needless to say, I didn't re-enlist anymore," he laughed.

During his first stint in the Navy, Kincaid served in a harbor defense unit in Norfolk, Virginia. He remained there for two years and finished his four-year stay in Providence, Rhode Island, where he was stationed on the *USS Lookout*, a radar picket ship that used radar to help defend the country's borders against missiles, planes, and enemy ships. "We'd spend thirty days out to sea and ten days in port," he says. "I spent two years on that ship, and it was very boring."

When Kincaid's first enlistment ended, he spent nearly two years out of the service. He married, obtained a job, and looked forward to a prosperous future. Then a naval incident occurred between the United States and North Vietnam in the Gulf of Tonkin that upset Kincaid very much. "I was sitting around watching television and the news came on about the attack in Tonkin. Something about that just got me thinking." After concluding that the

North Vietnamese were evidently crazy for attacking a U.S. warship, he said he decided, "I'm going to have to go help out." And he did. "I got patriotic and re-enlisted."

Kincaid admits that leaving his wife and family behind was difficult. "It was kind of hard. My wife didn't like it too well, but I had to go. Those people over there were crazy, and we had to do something about it."

Before traveling to Vietnam, however, the Navy sent their new re-enlistee to Coronado, California, for four weeks of jungle training and survival school. He also trained in Marine small arms and counter insurgency. "I learned about propaganda and how they [the North Vietnamese] work on your mind." Next was one week of prisoner-of-war camp. "I was beginning to believe I was a prisoner of war!" he laughs. "They would deprive you of water. You'd get about half a glass every day, and it'd cause your mind to go insane. The instructors were just like Communists. They would beat you, herd you around, and had us living in underground bunkers. It sure didn't seem like California."

Kincaid's next stop was Vietnam. His tour there lasted from February 1967 to February of 1968. When he first arrived, he remembers his orders being changed because the barge he was initially supposed to be on wasn't there. "We were just sitting around in Saigon getting in everybody's way," he says. Next, Kincaid was sent to Camron Bay for three weeks because there were barracks for him and the others in which to stay. Afterward, he found himself in Japan for three weeks filling the barge he was to be on with supplies. "It didn't have any main engines and had to be towed from Japan all the way to Vietnam," he recalls.

The ship on which Kincaid was stationed was a repair barge in the Mekong Delta, where U.S. Naval vessels often patrolled the rivers. His ship was a part of the Riverine Assault Force 117, Support Squadron 9. "There was fighting all around us, but I didn't go out on the patrol boats. When the patrol boats got blown up or torn up, I helped fix them back up." After repairs were made, Kincaid and the other members of his crew took the patrol boats out on the rivers to test them. "We didn't go very far—maybe a mile or two. We left the fighting up to the 9th Infantry Division. We transported them around."

Kincaid's official title on the repair barge was that of engineman, or more specifically, a diesel engine mechanic. When a fleet of ships came in needing repair, Kincaid remembers that orders were always to give them attention immediately. "We would work on them twenty-four hours around the clock. We did whatever it took to get the boats back out and ready for the next operation."

Kincaid remembers that when he first got on the barge, it was docked along a section of the Mekong River, where an American base was located.

"There were two companies of Army along with our barge. We were right out in the middle of nowhere." Kincaid stated that his barge was originally supposed to be part of a task force of naval ships that was to go up the river as part of a mission, but because the barge became stuck in the mud, the Navy just left it—as well as its crew—right there. About nine months later, Kincaid received the news that the ship in that he had originally been assigned had been blown up and destroyed. After that, he felt blessed to be stuck on a barge in the mud.

Although Kincaid never directly fought in combat, he recalls several occasions when the enemy mortared the barge; in addition, they received frequent bouts of sniper fire. "I'd sometimes sit around at night and watch them mortar the base. You could actually sit on the boat and watch the mortars fall on there," he says. "After that, I didn't have too much desire to get out there in the jungle." Because his ship was roughly a thousand yards from the base, Kincaid recalls the barge not getting much direct mortar fire, for it was too small of a target. It was difficult to find the people with the mortars, because once the Army reached the place from where they had come, the enemy would grab their mortar tubes and run. Before they ran away, however, the enemy usually discharged about eight to ten mortars. "You had no idea when they were coming or where they would hit," Kincaid says.

Kincaid recalled one particular night when a mortar attack occurred. "It was completely dark on the boat because at night all lights that could be seen were left off. I opened a door and began to watch the attack, and it was a good one. They were really after our butts. The next thing I knew, a mortar landed just to the side of our ship, and the second one landed directly on the other side. They just missed us. They sprayed water all over the ship. After that, I closed the door, because I figured the next mortar was going to be a direct hit. I was starting to try to figure out how I was going to get out of there."

That, however, was not the only time that enemy fire struck close to Kincaid. He remembers one instance when he and three or four of his buddies sat on the bank drinking a case of beer, which wasn't allowed on the ship. "It was pitch dark. The Army had a bunch of supplies—telephone poles, oil drums, and other things—there on the bank, and we were just sitting there among all that stuff. All of a sudden a sniper started shooting at us. He was probably a hundred yards away. I don't know how he could have seen us except maybe he saw us light our cigarettes."

He continued, "So we were just sitting there drinking a beer and smoking our cigarettes when all of a sudden we heard a small, flitting noise that was indistinct. We asked each other what it was, and then you could hear the bullets hitting the dirt. About this time an Army guy drove up in a Jeep with no lights and said, 'There's a sniper out here shooting at people. If you guys are smart, you'll get inside that ship.' We immediately got behind some telephone poles that were lying there. It was the first time I had ever heard a bullet go by me."

When Kincaid's second enlistment expired, he was ready to go home. "I knew that this war wasn't going to be over in no year or year and a half. I wasn't about to go back. At that time, machine gunners and enginemen kept getting rotated in and out of Vietnam, and I knew if I re-enlisted once again, I would have been going back."

Kincaid left Vietnam while the Tet Offensive took place. "All flights coming in and going out were cancelled, so I was sitting in Saigon trying to get out. Someone told me I could catch a cargo plane, but they had no idea where they were going. I got on one with the notion that I didn't care where it was going. I just wanted out of Vietnam." It ended up in Okinawa, and there Kincaid jumped on another cargo plane headed for Alaska. There he waited on another plane that eventually got him back to the continental U.S. Kincaid was finally home, where he has been ever since.

About the author.   Scott Scarberry is a life-long resident of Mason, West Virginia, where he lives with his mother, Arlene, and sister, Jodi. He is a senior at Wahama High School. When not in school, he likes hunting, fishing, and anything to do with the outdoors. He wishes to dedicate this story to his late grandfather, Bernard Scarberry.

Outraged by the Gulf of Tonkin incident, Eddie Kincaid re-enlisted in the Navy so he could be sent to Vietnam.

Lou MacEwan

United States Marine Corps
Korean War

By Randi Roush

In 1950, just five short years after being involved in the most tumultuous war in history, our Nation found itself once again in the position of sending our young men overseas. This time, the enemy was Communism, and the developing country of Korea was at stake. That same year, a twenty year-old Chicagoan named Lou MacEwan was just getting started with his adult life; however, in 1951, MacEwan felt the effects of a war on the other side of the world. In fact, he got drafted into it. Although this New Haven resident's contribution to UN efforts in Korea was significant, he enjoys stressing how his war experience helped him in his post-military life.

According to MacEwan, his selection into the Marine Corps as a result of the draft really came as no surprise. Perhaps the worst part of the process for him was the fact that he had just recently married. Before his assignment in Korea though, the young draftee completed basic training as well as cold weather training. After weeks of hard and tiring drills and preparing for what he would experience in a country half a world away, MacEwan boarded a ship to Korea. Right away, he received an assignment in supplies, and then found himself, when things got bad, volunteering in the infantry.

MacEwan talks very little about his combat experiences today, for his personality exudes optimism, and he cares not to regress back to bad experiences from what amounted to the hardest year of his life, which was how long he served in Korea. In fact, even after fifty years, it still proves difficult for MacEwan to talk about the painful and depressing memories that unfortunately remain in the recesses of his mind. "When people such as my children ask me questions about the war," he says, "I just simply reply, 'I survived one winter.'"

The harshness of that one cold winter in Korea, not to mention the human loss that it accompanied, has provided MacEwan with many memories. When it comes to war movies, he chooses not to watch them. "Why watch those kind of movies when I was there and actually experienced it?" he asks matter-of-factly.

MacEwan remembers vividly some of the dire living conditions faced by him and his peers. For example, as for sleeping, times existed when the soldiers had to lie in the open with their weapons while they slept. Food was, however, in supply around them for when they needed to eat. "You'll never know what it was like unless you were there," says MacEwan. Despite the memories of the war, MacEwan recounts the most frightening day as the one in which he arrived in Korea and disembarked the transport ship into landing craft. "I was scared every day I was there," he admits.

Each day in Korea was a struggle, according to MacEwan. "I came from a strong Christian family, and my faith is what kept me going," he said. "Every day I would pray." Growing up, he had come from a poor family. His dad left when MacEwan was two, and his mother worked hard to provide for them. For this reason, the family maintained a strong faith that God would continue to provide their needs. In Korea, MacEwan held onto this strong faith.

When his tour of duty ended, MacEwan returned home via San Francisco. He vividly recalls the sight of the Golden Gate Bridge, signifying his native land. And although he was thrilled to be home, MacEwan wishes that the military had done a better job of aiding him and his fellow veterans to re-adjust back to civilian life. "A priest or minister—someone—would have been nice to have been able to talk to, just to tell us about some of the little things we had missed; someone just to talk to us and give us an update as to what was going on in the United States." Along those lines, MacEwan offered some words of advice to everyone regarding the young men and women coming home from the present war. "Those kids will come home with a lot of problems," he said. "We all need to show them lots of compassion and do everything we can to try to help them adapt back to a normal life. They need to know that what they did is okay, and that they unfortunately had to do some things that maybe they weren't proud of at the time. There are things that have to bother you [war veterans] for a while, but then you have to get over it. You have to move on, but we need to help these boys and girls to figure that out."

Despite the hardship to MacEwan brought on by the war, he did the same thing as millions of other veterans—he pressed on, moved forward, and began to dream of a civilian lifestyle at home where he could live the American dream. And he did. "I feel so blessed because I had the greatest career," exclaimed MacEwan, and he wasn't talking great in terms of money. Instead, he spoke of fantastic experiences and incidents that provided tremendous excitement and travel around the world.

"I feel like I've never worked a day in my life," continued MacEwan. "When I came home from Korea, I took a night job in a factory. Every morning I went home, showered, put on a shirt and tie, and went looking for a sales job. By the time I was twenty-eight, I was a vice-president of sales and marketing. I retired from there when I was in my forties." MacEwan accomplished all of this after going to college for five years at night.

While working in marketing, MacEwan looks back on his career with much pride, but his eyes gleam brightest when talking about his best-known creation: the Ronald McDonald birthday parties at McDonald's restaurants. "I came up with the idea many, many years ago," said MacEwan.

MacEwan created a business selling birthday cakes, Danish, and batter to McDonald's. He eventually sold batters to Burger King and Long John Silver's also. As part of his duties as his company's president, he traveled around the globe—to sixty-eight countries all told. "One time I traveled to Thailand for a three-day meeting and loved it so much that I stayed a month. I've loved everywhere I've ever been, and I love where I'm at right now."

When asked if his travels ever included a return trip to Korea, MacEwan responded, "My wife made me go back there. I didn't recognize the place. There were these huge skyscrapers all around. It looked so different." MacEwan said he eventually sold his company, MacEwan Enterprises, in 1998. He credits the marketing field for much of his prosperity, and recommends it to young people today, especially females, who he says have tremendous opportunities today that didn't exist in decades past.

In addition to the pride he shows in his former business ventures, MacEwan displays an equal amount of pride in raising his four children, two boys and two girls. "I raised them and enjoyed every minute of it," he said. On March 29, 1980, he added other members to his family when he married his current wife, Carolyn, a Mason County native, and her three children. Together, they enjoy one another's company, along with getting to spoil their grandchildren.

MacEwan loves to relate the story of his post-war life to young people today. "They have so many opportunities if they'll just take advantage of them," he states. From growing up poor on the streets of Chicago to surviving the Korean War, MacEwan never gave up hope that life would someday become better, and today his life is a testament to everyone that dreams of better things. Today, MacEwan and Carolyn work hard to help local teens achieve dreams of their own through raising money for scholarships. At age seventy-eight, he has endured both cancer and heart disease, but just like with those traumatic incidents over a half century ago in Korea, not even health problems can stop Lou MacEwan. His story is one of inspiration for everyone.

Instead of reflecting upon his Korean War experiences, Lou MacEwan chooses to inspire young people to follow their dreams.

David W. "Bill" McFarland

United States Navy
World War II

By Hannah Foreman

Picture yourself one hundred miles out on the Atlantic Ocean, surrounded by clear blue water. Not only are the surroundings pleasant, but you are talking to some of the most interesting people you have ever met. This is what Bill McFarland experienced in the Atlantic Ocean in the 1940s. Unfortunately for him, this was no luxury vacation cruise, for he happened to have been serving as a Navy gunner on a merchant ship carrying supplies to aid the Allied cause in World War II.

McFarland grew up in the Bend Area of Mason County with his mother, father, and five brothers. Due to the effects of the Great Depression, the opportunity to graduate from high school did not present itself. Unable to attend school, McFarland instead worked several odd jobs to help support his family. He distinctly remembers husking corn around Christmas time in order to buy presents. Later, at the age of 22, McFarland was eager to learn and held a steady job at the TNT plant. He thought he had his whole life planned out. Then one day McFarland got frozen on the job (nowadays what is called being laid-off), and as a result made the decision to enlist in the United States Navy. When asked why he chose this particular branch, he replied, "I had good food, a dry place to sleep, and I was always around water anyway, and I liked it."

The period of time between McFarland's enlistment and his departure was a hasty one. He signed up on a Friday, and by the next Thursday he was on his way. McFarland recalls his father being very unsupportive, questioning his decision. In fact, the war years were extremely difficult for his parents, chiefly because over that span, all five of their sons eventually joined the service.

Instead of serving on traditional naval watercraft such as destroyers or aircraft carriers, the Navy instead stationed McFarland as a gunner on supply ships operated by the Merchant Marine. The majority of these ships was equipped with several large guns for protection and was manned by trained gunners from the Navy. McFarland recalls that oil was the most dangerous cargo on these ships. "You take eighteen thousand barrels of octane gasoline in the holds underneath of you, and imagine what a torpedo could do, and all of us on the ship would be gone. You wouldn't even have time to think about it."

As the chief gunner aboard ship, McFarland's chief responsibilities included checking all the guns on the vessel twice a day and making sure they were properly protected from the saltwater and sea air. "I had to make sure that those guns would work. That was my job. I'd also have to put my men on watch—four hours on and four hours off." McFarland had twenty-six servicemen under him. "I took pride in my work and loved every minute of it," McFarland says with a twinkle in his eyes.

Despite the heavy responsibilities that his job involved, McFarland recalls one light-hearted moment regarding guns on the ship. "We were docked in Scotland, and I didn't know the Queen of England didn't allow her birds to be shot. I had a .45 on my side, and I had to find out what it would do." Needless to say, McFarland chose to test his weapon out on a few seagulls. Even though he got into a little trouble with the ship's skipper, nothing serious ever came out of the situation, except, of course, for some funny memories.

Life in the Navy was somewhat comfortable. The servicemen were well fed with three hot meals a day. On the other hand, cramming four men into small sleeping quarters at once made for tight conditions. The gunmen resided in a separate section of the ship, away from the rest of the crew. They slept close to their stations in case of a surprise attack. Merchant ship crews were made up of average civilians mainly. McFarland describes the general emotions as being scared every time they slept.

McFarland's ship made several trips across the Atlantic carrying supplies for Allied troops, although he says he never really kept track of exactly how many. "Barring any bad storms, we arrived back in New York City about every forty-five days," he says. He enjoyed his time in New York, especially since his oldest brother was stationed there at the time. The ship often made stops in several Caribbean islands to load cargo before sailing for the Atlantic. "The island of Aruba contained nothing but gas wells on it. This was where we'd often pick our cargo up. While they put on the cargo, sometimes we got out the fishing gear. Then we'd go across the Atlantic, unload, and go through the entire process again." These trips to the Caribbean often provided some hair-raising experiences. "That sea was always littered with German subs. You could always find parts of ships floating around that they had destroyed. Our skipper never wanted to wait for the convoys down there."

Another close call occurred in 1944. He describes this day as the most vivid in his mind. "We were traveling through a foreign port, and our engine went out. This seemed like a minor problem to the average mechanic, but this was not the case with a time limit of only seventy-two safe hours hanging over your head." The British cruisers followed them as they coasted along without an engine. The captain realized their situation wasn't going to improve, so he sent all married men ashore. The captain and the single men stayed by the ship's side to defend against the enemy. After several failed attempts to escape the opposition, they all reached a fatal end. Realizing they were fighting a losing battle, the men ended their assault and committed suicide. Thankfully for McFarland, he was married and had been one of the men sent ashore.

However, it was one particular voyage across the Atlantic that gave McFarland the scare of his life. Usually, the ships traveled in large convoys because there was strength in numbers. Unfortunately, that didn't always scare away U-boats, or German submarines. McFarland remembers: "We were all doing our daily tasks around mid-day when I heard a bullhorn blast. As soon as I heard the sound, my heart jumped to my throat because you see, a noise like that can only mean one thing." As he raised his head from the job, he was taken back by three German destroyer escorts traveling toward his ship at ten knots. The next forty-five minutes were the longest of McFarland's life as the Germans dropped "ash cans." All huddled together, McFarland's crew regained formation. The U.S. merchant ship saw this as a chance to prove its strength, so all men rushed to their stations. On each side of the ship, designated men pressed a button and released fire on the Germans. Because they all had pretty good aim, it wasn't long before this focused crew destroyed the U-boat and turned back the remaining German ships.

Although McFarland does not tell of any stories regarding combat with the Germans, he recalls encountering German prisoners. "We had German prisoners serving us meals when we were at camp waiting to get our discharges. They were just like us though. They were safe and they knew it." McFarland said the prisoners wore white uniforms with the letters "P-W" on the backs. "That was in case they had to be identified if they escaped, but they didn't want to escape. They had a warm bed and were glad to be where they were."

On November 20, 1945, McFarland received his honorable discharge from the service after more than three years of duty. Looking back, he harbors no regrets in enlisting in the Navy and says that he remains to this day happy about his decision. He recalls his happiest moments as the ones when he was given liberty off the ship. One day while on liberty, he and a friend met and conversed with two British soldiers. These men had plenty to talk about, for they understood each other's struggles. "The British seemed thankful, but the Frenchmen, they were just nasty to us," McFarland revealed, crossly. McFarland and his shipmates, however, were ordered to be very cautious about what they said while away from the ship on liberty. "Our orders were that whenever you went on liberty, you never told how many men you had aboard ship, what ship you're on, and when you're figuring on sailing or anything like that. You'd get locked up if you did."

Another memorable time on liberty, and probably the most notable, was during a journey to New York City. McFarland was visiting Pier 90 and the Empire State Building. He was staying at the same hotel as an attractive young lady named Anna. They met during that time, and it didn't take long for them to hit it off. After dating for a while, the couple married in 1943 while McFarland was yet in the Navy. After the war, the couple added two boys to their family, Charlie and Raymond.

Bill McFarland's Navy experience, in his opinion, was a very good one. He cannot begin to count the number of countries and islands he visited during his military years, and his service time allowed him the opportunity to gain valuable training that aided him later in life. Now a widower, this eighty-eight year-old New Haven resident occupies a modest home in New Haven, West Virginia, with his dog, Maggie. Some of his favorite pastimes are mowing the grass and gardening. When people ask him his age or about his health, he shows his sense of humor by replying, "What do you mean how am I doing? I'm 29 and holding."

Bill McFarland served in World War II as a
Naval gunner aboard a Merchant Marine ship.

Bill Pauley

United States Army Air Corps
World War II

By Tory Raynes

When World War II comes to the minds of Americans today, they usually think of key land battles like those fought in France, Saipan, and Iwo Jima. However, some of the fiercest combat in both the European and Pacific Arenas occurred in the air, where fighter planes and bombers patrolled the skies. American aircraft were key in both protecting ground forces and performing assaults from high above. One World War II veteran who knows all about these important air tactics is Bill Pauley, who served on a B-17 bomber in Europe.

After completing his first semester at Marshall College (now Marshall University), Pauley began feeling mixed emotions regarding his future. "I'd say my friends influenced me the most when it came down to joining the military," he states. "I finally gave in and enlisted in the fall of '42." Pauley joined the Army Air Corps, known today as the Air Force, which sent him almost immediately to Fort Thomas in Kentucky for the induction part of the enlistment. "When I boarded the train in Charleston, there were only six other boys on it," he says. Those six men happened to be some of Pauley's classmates from high school.

On November 2nd at 2:00 P.M., as Pauley and his buddies laid around on their bunks, a sergeant entered. "I want Private Pauley to gather all his belongings and be ready in thirty minutes," the sergeant commanded. A few hours later, Pauley boarded a train to Fresno, California, for eight weeks of basic training. "It was rough, just like I knew it would be. I didn't get much sleep, and I recall being very sore." Pauley pulled through it though, and after two months the Air Corps sent him to Denver for aero-gunnery school. After a stop in Los Angeles for weather school, Pauley attended two additional schools for communication and radio operation. Little did he know at the time that the Air Corps was preparing him for a huge responsibility aboard a B-17 bomber.

After months of training, Pauley's outfit, the Ninety-sixth Bomb Group, 413th Bomb Squadron, and D Flight, finally departed overseas for the European Theater of Operations. They headed to Snetterton, England, where they would be stationed.

On November 29, 1943, the members of the outfit put what they had learned to work when they set out on their first mission. "There were ten gun positions on B-17 F-models. These planes had been retro-fitted for radar." Pauley explained that B-17's usually held ten people. "You had four commissioned officers: your pilot, who was the crew commander; a co-pilot, who was the second in command; a navigator; and a bombardier. Then there were six non-commissioned officers, which consisted of me, a radio operator." In addition to manning the radio, Pauley operated one fifty-caliber flexible gun.

Pauley's missions during the war proved very interesting. Every day the crew looked at the mission board schedule to check their target for that day. "Our targets were mostly manufacturing sites. You wanted to shoot for the primary and alternate targets. The whole purpose was to take Hitler out of business."

Being a radio operator, Pauley's job consisted of telling the navigator their plane's location along with where it needed to be. "The whole course was laid out for us, so we knew everything." Although they knew everything, someone still watched from the ground, aware of their location at all times; in fact, every couple of minutes they received an automatic phone call to check on the crew and make sure they were safe in the air.

The goal for the Ninety-sixth Bomb Group was to get forty B-17's in formation, which didn't always happen. After the planes gained formation, the American fighter planes and the British escorted them to Germany, where most of their missions were conducted. "The Brits were very gracious," Pauley exclaims. However, the Germans did attack them a few times. The Nazis had great radars, thus making it difficult to hide from them. When a German plane would hit them, Pauley and the crew were ready. "We sat on our parachutes," he laughs. "And get this—we wore long-johns under our uniforms. It was so cold that we didn't want to be stranded somewhere with barely any clothes on."

Pauley remembers his second mission very clearly. "In December '43 we flew to North Africa. The German General Rommel was running all over that area. I'm not really sure why the Allies sent bombers in—maybe it was for a psychological effect—but we made that trip and came back to England."

Pauley laughs at what his pilot named their plane—"Contrary Mary." In fact, there were actually three Contrary Mary's on which Pauley flew a total of thirty-two missions. The first two were destroyed in combat. "On the first one, we were just coming from a bombing mission over Berlin. We lost the superchargers on two engines, and we had severe hydraulic damage. We were shot all to pieces. All I had on the radio was the emergency wave, so I couldn't communicate with any other aircraft. I could just barely communicate with the crew." Luckily, Pauley and the other members of the crew kept the plane up long enough to reach the English Channel.

"The Good Lord certainly played a great part in our survival," he continues. "We could see the Channel, and all of a sudden I got this radio signal." The signal came from the Royal Air Force's air-sea rescue. Since Pauley himself had been unable to get a signal up until this time, he explained that evidently another plane had reported the trouble they were experiencing. "I got the signal from a British pilot—a girl. She was flying air-sea rescue services." The British used many female pilots at this time for these specific purposes.

"Suddenly," continued Pauley, "I had voice communication with her, and she said, 'I'll follow you in. Just set it down on its tail.'" She then told Pauley to inform the crew that upon landing in the Channel to get out of the plane, and she would send someone to pick them up. "The Colonel set that thing down on its tail, and it made a loud noise. We opened every hatch we had on it to get out, and then we got the crew raft out and inflated." Pauley says that the tail-gunner, Joe Hahn, was the last man out of the plane. He laughs when he recalls that Hahn fell out of the raft into the English Channel. The British did indeed pick them up and took them back to the designated point where they were to meet if their missions were ever aborted.

After Pauley's twenty-fifth mission in May, the Army permitted him to come home for thirty days. Afterward, he traveled to Kansas, where he participated in B-29 training until December. "I didn't like B-29's because I was so used to B-17's, but they were great planes." With B-29 training finally over, Pauley returned to England to fly more missions.

On the downside, Pauley said his saddest memory about the war was when his pilot died. "Being together so much, we all became close friends, so it was definitely sad when he passed, but he'll always be remembered," states Pauley.

The base in Great Britain featured both an officer's section and an enlister's section. However, the men didn't always stay there. For instance, every seventh mission the crew was granted leave. They traveled everywhere in groups, including Scotland and London. In fact, Pauley could go anywhere he wanted on free days as long as he had money. The Royal British Hotel would let the American flyers stay for free, and the English people also invited them into their homes. When asked what they did for fun, Pauley simply replied, "Chased girls!" Some U.S. airmen even attended college classes at the famed Cambridge University.

Even though Pauley said the food wasn't bad, he and his best friend Joe (the one who fell off the raft) share some very fond memories about their meals. It seems that Joe was notorious for sneaking food into his bags that he carried wherever he went. This let him become very good friends with chefs at many of the hotels. "Ole Joe would take his bag of food into the hotel, and the chef would cook it for us," laughs Pauley. "It was definitely better than eating that old powered stuff."

In November 1945, Pauley received his discharge and was free to come home. Upon his arrival, he started working and soon after met his soul mate. They later married in 1946. "I joined the reserves shortly after that," says Pauley. "I had a good chance of making master sergeant." The Army recalled Pauley on July 4, 1951, sending him to Andrews Air Force Base. Luckily, he just missed being sent to serve in the Korean War. At Andrews he learned all about what went on in the reserves and about new equipment. Soon enough, Pauley reached his goal of making master sergeant. That December when his reserve was up, the Army discharged him.

Now with four children, seven grandchildren, and one great-grandson, Pauley lives life to its fullest potential. He and his wife have now been married sixty-three years, and he celebrated his eighty-fifth birthday this year. "I guess it was the Good Lord who got me through that rough patch in my life," says the teary-eyed Pauley.

*Bill Pauley served as a radio operator aboard B-17 bombers in the European
Theatre of Operations during World War II.*

Kevin Peters

United States Marine Corps
Operation Iraqi Freedom

By Deidra Peters

Anyone who has ever served his or her country inside a war zone knows that it is difficult to ever feel safe. For Iraq War veteran Kevin Peters, even meal time often had its dangers. In fact, Peters says that he and his friend sat down for dinner one evening when surprisingly out of nowhere, incoming rockets started exploding. This as well as many other incidents stands out in the mind of Peters as he recalls his two tours of duty.

Born in 1971, Peters grew up in Clifton, West Virginia. With three older siblings picking on him, orneriness definitely existed as a dominant personality trait. "Growing up with him was great," said his older brother, Steve. "Just all of us kids would sometimes maybe do something that we knew our dad would be furious about; then we would hide it from him." However, Kevin, the youngest child of Carol and Lewis Peters, says that throughout his childhood he had always wanted to join the Marines, and he fulfilled that dream on July 26, 1989.

Both of his parents as well as other family members were proud to see him accomplish his goals. "I felt I could really make a difference," states Peters, "and I wanted to do something more with my life." After several years of dedication to the Marine Corps, he joined the Army National Guard and settled down to start his family in 2000.

The following year, the world changed as terrorists attacked New York City's World Trade Center Towers. As a result, Peters, then thirty-two, was called into active service and sent to Iraq to take part in the War on Terrorism. When his family found out, they worried and feared for him, but despite the apprehension, Peters knew he had a job to do. Within a couple of months the military stationed him in the strategic city of Fallujah.

When asked what his typical days were like in Iraq, Peters replied, "Everything from good to horrible. At one time I actually had a room. On the other hand, I also slept in a culvert with dirt and mud, not to mention other stuff." His daily routine usually varied. "Different missions called for different activities. Some mornings, there wouldn't be much to do, whereas others you couldn't seem to get everything done." Checking weapons and performing pre-combat inspections were daily rituals, as well as checking ammunition. Peters usually carried a double amount of combat ammo, about two hundred and ten rounds. Grenades were also a necessity. In addition, communication systems had to be checked.

The first time Peters was sent to Iraq, his major job was to repair electronics equipment for the military. He also escorted convoys from base to base. These convoys carried food, fuel, and supplies. "Beans, bullets, and band-aids—all the necessities that we needed," he laughed.

Weather certainly played a major role when attempting to perform a task in Iraq. Peters remembers days when the temperature reached above one hundred and forty degrees during the hottest part of the year. "It caused you to not feel like eating much more than breakfast," he says.

Speaking of eating, Peters recalls one particular incident involving meal time: "I had a pretty good friend over there named Josh Searls, who is also from Mason County. He asked me to go to evening chow with him, so I went, and no sooner had we gotten our meal and sat down that rockets and mortars started to hit all over the area." Everyone threw themselves onto the floor to minimize the chance of catching shrapnel. As soon as the rockets and mortars stopped, they took their food and dumped it. A head count was then taken to account for all soldiers on post.

Peters and Searls' adventures during chow didn't stop there, however. The next time they ate together, the same thing happened. In fact, it happened five times when the two attempted to eat with one another. "I finally told him, 'I'm never eating with you again,'" he laughs, "and I didn't—at least not while we were there." They occasionally get together now and talk, and they can eat with one another in peace.

Things were worse for Peters during his second stint in Iraq. "The living conditions were about the same. We had just started operations in Sader City, and there wasn't any base there, so we built our own. We were living by the seat of our pants, really." During this second tour, Peters' major job was as a signal support systems specialist.

Peters did say that the second time he was dispatched to Iraq, the country was at least in better shape. "It just happened, though, that I got put in one of the worst spots in the country. I was stuck in one of the last places with heavy resistance." Just because he had been in the country once before did not necessarily make time go by any faster either. "It actually went slower. "I think the main reason was because I was getting so tired of what I was doing." Peters mentioned that during this tour, he suffered a bout with depression because a very close friend was killed. "While going over, I thought nothing bad would happen to me, but after my friend died, I just couldn't believe it. I realized that it could have been me." Peters himself came close to death on several occasions. Mortars, rockets, and roadside bombs provided many close calls.

Throughout his military experience, Peters says he encountered many cases where he saw combat. Of course, it almost always occurred at the most surprising moments. According to Peters, "It's an indescribable experience because it happens so fast. Something that may normally take you three to five seconds might take you fifteen seconds." As an example of what he meant by this, he cited how long it seemed to take when reloading his rifle.

The worst part of both tours of duty for Peters was leaving behind his family. During his first departure, he left his pregnant wife, Bonita, and two small sons, Trey, then three, and Wesley, who was one. His third son was born during Peters' first deployment to Iraq.

One colorful recollection that Peters has about his time in Iraq involved a small creature called a camel spider. "They would walk in your shadow to try to avoid the heat. You thought they were chasing you, but they were really just trying to stay cool." He recalls them being about the size of a human hand.

The war definitely affected Peters' outlook on life. He realized how quickly life could end and learned to say a thing like "I love you" while he has the chance. He also thoroughly enjoys spending time with his family. "I value the time I have with family and friends," he says.

Like most veterans, Peters says that although many bad memories exist from his time in Iraq, he would do it all over again if given the chance. "I enjoyed being a part of what our country was doing," he explains. In addition, Peters fondly remembers the heartfelt mail and care packages he received from numerous people, schools, and groups back home. "They really helped bring me out of being depressed after a friend was killed."

For his service to our country, Peters earned several awards and medals, such as a Sea Service Deployment Ribbon, Bronze Star Medal, Army Commendation Medal, US Navy Achievement Medal, Army Good Conduct Metal, Marine Corps Good Conduct Medal, and a Combat Action Badge, just to name a few.

When returning back from the war, Peters found it hard to adjust to his old routines. He was used to waking up early every morning and carrying out his daily rituals. But upon returning home, he had different responsibilities. The first time coming home he had to tend to his newborn child, and the second time he just had to be a dad. It was like he had to retrain himself in order to adjust back to civilian life.

Peters recently left a job at the Department of Defense and now works at Gavin Power Plant in Cheshire, Ohio. Today he lives in Point Pleasant, West Virginia, and spends every spare second with his family. With his oldest son at the age of eight and the youngest at the age of four, they keep him pretty busy. Peters enjoys going camping with his brother's and sisters' families. He says that anytime you can be with family and friends, it is great. One thing is for sure—at least he can sit down to dinner today without mortars and rockets!

About the Author. Deidra Renee Peters currently lives in Clifton, West Virginia, with her parents and three siblings. Most of her time is dedicated to sports or keeping up with school work. She now holds the position of vice-president in the National Honor Society. Deidra also enjoys spending time with her close friends, Hannah and Jon, and going on family camping trips. Her future plans after graduating consist of going to college and pursuing a degree in the medical field.

After several years serving in the Marine Corps, Kevin Peters joined the National Guard, which sent him to Iraq as part of Operation Iraqi Freedom.

Harry "Chub" Pickens

United States Merchant Marine
World War II

By Robert Zerkle

In 1939 a conflict between nations occurred that forever impacted the history of the world: World War II. The United States entered two years later with the Japanese attack on Pearl Harbor. The day after, all military branches prepared troops, planes, and ships to be sent to Japan and Europe. Among them was the Merchant Marine. Although they seldom get recognized for their contributions, this group of men played a very integral part in the U.S. war efforts. Their main duties included carrying supplies and transporting American military men. One local man who enlisted in the Merchant Marine was Harry "Chub" Pickens of New Haven.

When Pickens joined the Merchant Marines in 1945, he was just seventeen years of age. "I had to get special permission from my parents," he says. "In fact, I was still in high school at the time." Pickens traveled to Cincinnati to enlist, and when he graduated from Wahama, he had already been sworn in. Pickens says that at the time, the Merchant Marine was a division of the Coast Guard and was not recognized as a service branch. "When you enlisted, you actually went into what was called the Maritime Service, which was basically being part of the crew of a ship."

As for the reason why Pickens joined, he states, "It was right toward the end of World War II, and I wanted to do something. I knew that if you went into the Army or the Navy, you'd be in training until the war ended. I didn't want to miss out on anything." Pickens continued by saying that by May of that year, the war with Germany had ended, but the battle in the Pacific loomed on. "I had two friends that had joined the Merchant Marines and had seen the world, and I wanted to do the same thing."

Just like the regular service, Pickens and the other new Merchant Marine members began their tenures in boot camp just outside of Brooklyn, New York. This lasted only about three weeks. Pickens remembered boot camp as being fairly easy. "They weren't too rough on us. We had to drill, take swimming lessons, pull guard duty, and all the things that the other services did." He recalled that he wore fatigues similar to those worn in the Navy. When his three weeks ended, his superiors assigned him to a ship.

According to Pickens, after boot camp the Merchant Marine would ask for volunteers to go into particular jobs. Pickens volunteered for the steward department. He almost immediately was assigned to a ship in Boston, and they gave him a job as a waiter in the officers' dining room. "When the servicemen were on the ship, we had to serve them meals. I did that for several months."

As for the terms of service in the Merchant Marine, they were a little different from the branches of the military. "We signed contracts saying that we agreed to make a particular voyage. If you then wanted to sail on that ship again, then you had to re-sign." Pickens signed on to the same ship for the most part of 1945.

Although Pickens' first voyage aboard his ship was apart from other vessels, his remaining trips overseas were as a member of a convoy. "They wouldn't let one ship at this time go alone," he says. This was right after the war with Germany had ended, and traveling as part of a convoy provided strength in numbers. Most of his voyages consisted of trips back and forth from France to New York City. "Our docks were just off Twenty-Second Street in New York," he says.

Among other experiences on the ship, Pickens states that he and the other men shared some good times in between the many hours of work. To unwind, they mainly played cards. The ship also offered its sailors a recreation room, where there were ping-pong tables and other forms of activities. He recalls even going to a high school in France on one occasion to play basketball. As for food, Pickens says he was fed very well on board the ship. "The food was actually very good. As a waiter, I often got the same first-class food as the officers."

Another pleasurable activity occurred when the ship reached port in France. Pickens and the others would leave the ship and explore. "You were free when you got to port over there. Unfortunately, you were only usually in port for a day or two. I traveled around quite a bit, but I never got to Paris." Pickens did say that he and some of his fellow crewmen once made a trip into Germany.

Pickens says that quite a bit of camaraderie existed among the ship's crew. In fact, because of his job, Pickens was often in close contact with the ship's officers. At one time, he had a job known by those on the ship as the "Captain's boy." He says, "You took care of the Captain. You served the meals at the Captain's table, which contained the first six officers on the ship. I had to oftentimes take Captain Anderson's meals to him up on the bridge, where they did the navigation. I'd have to do that three times a day." In addition, this job entitled him to several privileges. "When you went to port and the captain left the ship, that meant you were free."

When asked what kinds of cargo that the ships in which he sailed carried, Pickens replied that they mainly carried troops back to the United States. "I was on an Army troop ship. We were actually paid by the Army, and we would go from the United States to France and pick up American soldiers who had fought in the war. Our ship wasn't a big one, but we usually carried about three thousand troops." Although neither Pickens nor any of his fellow crewmen carried any arms, each Merchant Marine ship had a gun crew consisting of naval gunners.

Pickens remembers one specific voyage extremely well. One time his ship sailed to France to pick up war brides, women who U.S. soldiers had married while in Europe. "We had to put the ship in dry dock in order to prepare it for women." There were about four hundred of these war brides coming to the United States on this particular voyage.

After approximately ten trips to Europe, Pickens boarded a ship in New York headed to the Pacific. It too was a troop transport, holding nearly ten thousand people. "We went through the Panama Canal, into the Pacific, and to the Philippine Islands. We island-hopped all the way there, including stops in Guam and Japan. This was after the atomic bomb had been dropped. Everything was flat, and they were starting to clean up." On the way back, Pickens was privileged to make a stop in Hawaii.

When it came to communication, Pickens kept in touch with his family quite frequently, mostly by letters, but sometimes by telephone. However, once out of the Merchant Marine, Pickens lost contact with most of the friends he had made and thus never really communicated with them after his tenure ended.

Because Pickens came in toward the end of the war, none of the ships on which he was stationed was ever under attack. "When you traveled on these ships, they had what they called 'war zones,' which for the most part were all around Europe. The first trip that I made, which was to France, was considered inside a war zone, even though the war in Europe was technically over." Pickens was aboard a ship when the war officially ended. "There was total jubilation."

Pickens says he really has no regrets in regard to joining the Merchant Marine, even at such a young age. However, he did say, "At one time I had wanted to join the Navy, but it seemed like circumstances didn't allow me to do it." He even thought about enlisting after his term in the Merchant Marine had ended, but by this time he had married. By the time the Korean War ended, Pickens and all five of his brothers had served in the military during wartime: John (Army), Richard (Marines) and Chub during World War II; and Bill (Navy), Ray (Army), and Jack (Army) during the Korean War.

After his terms of service ended, Pickens bounced around at several jobs, but in 1950 he went to work for American Electric Power's Phillip Sporn Plant in New Haven, where he spent thirty-nine years. In 1996, a half a century after Pickens' service, Congress passed legislation recognizing those who had served in the Merchant Marine as official war veterans, a moment that made Pickens very proud.

About the Author. Robert Zerkle was born in Point Pleasant, West Virginia, and currently lives next to the Ohio River in New Haven, West Virginia. In his spare time he likes to race quads at the Mason County Fair Grounds on the weekends. He plans on continuing welding classes in high school to become a boilermaker.

Eager to become involved in World War II, Harry "Chub" Pickens enlisted in the Merchant Marine at age seventeen in 1945.

Dennis Rayburn

United States Army National Guard
Operation Iraqi Freedom

By Nathan Stewart

Dennis Rayburn steps to the podium inside the Wahama High School classroom with great confidence. For this lecture, he has prepared a presentation titled "The Military Effect" regarding the repercussions of combat to the psyches of the men and women who represented this country in battle. As he speaks, it is easily observed that the welfare of his military brothers and sisters is important to him, for there exists extreme passion in his voice. Being a war veteran himself, Rayburn is vastly knowledgeable about his subject.

In 1978, Dennis Rayburn enlisted into the United States Army National Guard at the age of twenty-four. He knew about the challenges that he would face in the training camps and definitely on the battlefield, but he did not care because he wanted to serve his country. The first days provided more of a challenge than he expected. He was sent to Fort Jackson in South Carolina to undergo his preparation drills for battle. "The first days of training were the most frightening days of my life," exclaims Sergeant First Class Retired Rayburn. He was taught to understand the importance of being a soldier, to do what the superiors say, and to respect your equals, even if you do not like them personally. "These life lessons should be taught in our schools," says Rayburn with great sincerity. He also learned the fundamentals of combat: how to use a gun with great accuracy, how to never leave a soldier in need, and how to react when unarmed. "If you do not know these in the battlefield, you are as good as dead," Rayburn says with great knowledge in his voice.

In the years that followed basic training Rayburn had several opportunities to travel the world. He was sent to Germany, where he said most soldiers have a good time because there is a lot of beer. He did not participate in the drinking as much as most, but he did at least sample the foreign brews. "The beer was served in liter-sized steins served by women who carried the elixir four per hand without spilling a single drop," he said, amazed at how strong these women were. "They were more precise than most men," Rayburn said. "They could withstand great stress and act as if it was nothing."

On September 11, 2001, at the age of forty-seven, Rayburn was working in the West Virginia National Guard Combined Support Maintenance Facility and listening to the radio. He heard that America was under attack and was horribly shocked like everyone else in the United States that day. "This was one of the most significant things to ever happen in my life," Rayburn said with sadness in his voice. He was so hurt that he wanted to do something about it, desiring to fight whoever was responsible, even though he was perhaps a little too old. He resolved then to do whatever he could, not caring at the time of the dangers in such a terrible environment.

In 2004, Rayburn was sent to Iraq to fight in Operation Iraqi Freedom. Almost immediately, he witnessed the horrors of war. For example, while traveling in a convoy he recalled seeing the burnt out hulls of many American vehicles on the side of the road. These were the result of improvised explosive devices, IED's. "Can you imagine looking away for just a second, the vehicle in front of you explodes and is gone before your eyes?" Rayburn asks. He praised God that that had not been him in those flaming death traps. "I was very lucky to have not been blown away in such a manner," he spoke with relief. "God must have had plans for me. I am quite relieved that I am still alive."

While in Iraq, he did have some time to relax; he tried the food in the regions of Iraq in which he had been and did whatever else he could. "The food was quite different; they served a lot of goat and bread and stuff," Rayburn said. "What they served in the mess hall was excellent compared to the stuff the natives had. I never developed a taste for Middle Eastern food. Most of the soldiers ate MREs (Meals Ready to Eat); however, they did sometimes eat in the mess hall," Rayburn stated. While on leave, Rayburn enjoyed reading world history. "Without the knowledge of things that has happened, we will more than likely repeat whatever that may be," he said. "I do not know why people are not more aware of events that happened in the past which could help them prevent future disaster," he stated, realizing the dangers of which many go through because of their own arrogance. "I had several in my platoon that I thought were going to shoot me down accidentally. Some fellow combatants did not know the value of team work. They had no idea of the things that were going on around them. They could have learned a few lessons from the history of past battles."

One hot day at the Al Taqaddum Air Base a few miles away from Al Fallujah, SFC Rayburn had a terrible feeling within his chest, a quite painful sensation. He was experiencing a heart attack. The stresses in the battle zone caused him to become susceptible, he believes. Luckily for Rayburn, one of his friends from Mason County, Travis Gray, was accompanying him on that day. "Travis stayed with me until help arrived," said Rayburn, "and I'm grateful to him to this day." Rayburn and Gray remain great friends.

Rayburn continued, "I was first sent from the air base to Baghdad and then to Germany, where I spent eight days recuperating. Then I was sent to the Walter Reed Army Medical Center in the United States," he said, talking about his painful journey. While in the Baghdad hospital, Rayburn had thoughts that he had already died because he awoke in the same room as those who were severely wounded and appeared dead because they were unconscious and awaiting evacuation. "I wanted out of there. The costs of war were too great to see," noted Rayburn in great remembrance.

When his service in the war ended, he did not call it quits with the military. For instance, he now works for AMVETS as the State Commander. AMVETS is an abbreviation for American Veterans, a non-profit organization that aids veterans in getting what they need after their duties have ended. As a State Commander, he represents these veterans personally. He does a lot of paper work to make sure they get the help they so dearly deserve and not be treated like the veterans after the Vietnam War. The help that is given often includes financial assistance and health-related assistance. "I am one that they can come to when they need help, whether it be when they are seriously wounded or healthy," stated Rayburn while asked about his duties. He is an extremely valuable advocate when it comes to veterans in need.

With all of his experiences, the military awarded him quite a few medals over his career. Among his awards he received three which he cherishes: the Humanitarian Medal, the Army Excellence in Competition Badge, and the Air Force Recognition Award, which is very strange because he was part of the Army and not the Air Force. He was also honored with many more citations, but these are the three that truly define him.

A very philosophical person, Rayburn finds reason in everything. He reads to understand his history, unlike most men who just live for today. Benjamin Franklin is one of the many great sources that had many old proverbs that Rayburn greatly prefers to use in his everyday life. Franklin stated, "The man who trades freedom for security does not deserve nor will he ever receive either." Rayburn explained, "When not properly trained, people tend to surrender their rights for their security. When you surrender your rights for your security, you get security without any rights." Rayburn likes to say, "Everyone should know to not give their rights and not to let others keep you from reaching your goals. Irrational people make irrational decisions when confronted by a challenge, which can change their lives forever."

Dennis Rayburn served his country during war time at an age when most men and women feel past their primes. This goes quite a long way toward not only showing his love for his country, but it also defines the type of person that he is. Today he continues to carry on this same spirit through the work he performs in service of fellow veterans. He truly typifies what it means to be an American patriot.

About the Author. Nathan L. Stewart is a senior at Wahama High with great intentions on becoming a big success. He enjoys listening to music and playing the guitar. When he is not buried in the books, he enjoys helping people when they are in need of assistance. Also being quite knowledgeable, Nathan takes pleasure in the philosophies and the prophecies of long ago.

As a guest speaker, Dennis Rayburn helps to prepare Mr. Rayness's students for the interview process of this project.

Ershel "Bill" Riffle

United States Army Air Corps
World War II Veteran

By Sam German

As an airman in the Army Air Corps during World War II, Bill Riffle of New Haven never fired a single shot at the enemy, nor was he ever fired upon; yet his role as an expert instructor and gunman on B-29 bombers was extremely instrumental in the victorious outcome of the Allied forces in the Pacific Arena, for through his efforts B-29 pilots and crewmen were better prepared and protected to carry out their perilous missions.

While at his home in Leon, West Virginia, one day, Riffle, then eighteen, received his draft letter in 1943. "At the time you couldn't enlist," said Riffle, "because everything was frozen. You had to wait your turn. I received this letter, and I was very happy, but I wasn't happy that they pulled me out of the tenth grade. I never had the opportunity to finish my schooling."

Riffle recalls vividly how he received an assignment in the Army Air Corps: "I was sent to Fort Thomas, Kentucky. There they would call out our names on a P.A. system, our branch of service, and also where our next camp would be. There was a camp in Indiana, and if you got sent there, it meant you were in the infantry. I knew I didn't want to go there." One night the person on the loud speaker blared out: "Bill Riffle, Air Force, St. Petersburg, Florida." Riffle says, "When I heard my name and that I was going to be in the Air Force, I jumped up and danced around the room until the other men with me could not hear the loud speaker." Not only had Riffle avoided the infantry, but he had always wished to fly in planes.

Training in the Air Force was far from rigorous, according to Riffle. In fact, his actual training in St. Petersburg lasted only seven days in a place known as "tent city." Riffle states, "Everything there was literally tents, as far as you could see—from the mess hall to the latrines." In fact, the worst part of training was the latrines, mainly because in order to get in he would have to be wearing his entire uniform, complete with leggings and gas mask.

Although these living conditions sound harsh, Riffle credits his ease in adapting to this environment to his year away from home in the Civilian Conservation Corps as a teenager, where the camps were just as primitive. The Civilian Conservation Corps, or CCC, was a work relief program during the Great Depression under Franklin Roosevelt's New Deal. Many of the routines and acts of discipline in the Air Force resembled what Riffle endured in the CCC.

After a quick stop for some additional training in Clearwater, Florida, Riffle moved on to airplane mechanics school in Gulfport, Mississippi. Later, Riffle spent time at an airplane electrical school in Illinois. The next stop in his training process was Seattle, Washington, where the Boeing Company built aircraft for the military. While here Riffle received his most specialized training. Finally, his last training stop was Denver, Colorado, at Lowery Air Force Base Number 2, where he received armament training with 50-caliber and 20-mm machine guns. At the end of his schooling, he was a qualified engineer on B-29s, B-17s, and C-47s. All told, he spent thirteen months being educated by the Air Force. All of this schooling helped optimize his abilities to know what always occurred with the airplanes at all times.

In 1944 the Air Force and Boeing introduced Riffle to the B29 bomber, which at the time was the Air Force's best-kept secret. "The B29s were so secret at that time that the armor [the guns] was totally covered up. Although we got to go inside of them, we didn't even get to see them on the outside at first." B29 bombers became the most sophisticated bomber planes in the world very quickly, according to Riffle. "They were built much larger so they could carry around more bombs. They also had a greater amount of fire power, with two large bomb bays."

In Seattle, the Air Force made Riffle what they called a flight instructor as well as a qualified engineer. After nearly thirteen months of schooling, Riffle said that the Air Force felt they had invested so much time in his education that they resisted sending him overseas into combat. Once trained in the intricacies of the B29, Riffle and his crewmates were responsible for training other crews to fly these planes into combat zones for bombing raids in the Pacific. "All of the crews that I trained went to Saipan. I mainly taught those boys how to use the guns aboard the plane, along with the bailout procedure. Most of the boys I trained were young and green, and many of them went over there [to the Pacific] and got killed." So that he could better train other crews, Riffle often flew in the B29s himself. This to him was the best part of his everyday routine while in Seattle.

Although going up in planes was what seemed to Riffle to be the best thing to wake up and do every day, it wasn't always pleasant. On one morning, for instance, he awoke to what seemed to be a routine day as a gunner. After putting on his uniform and getting ready for what lay ahead, he traversed to the air strip. Boarding the plane and settling down proceeded as planned, but upon take-off, Riffle observed the number two engine, which to his surprise was on fire. The flames spanned clear back to the rear of the plane. Unfortunately for Riffle and the rest of the crew, the pilot could not immediately land. Ironically enough, the plane needed to gain altitude in order to get back on pattern with the runway. This unfortunately took twenty-five minutes. Riffle says, "I wasn't really scared when this happened because we all knew we were taking a huge risk when getting into the planes, so it really didn't worry me." Once the plane landed, the crew inspected the damages and discovered they had landed not a moment too soon because the flames had nearly spread to the fuel tanks.

A second bad experience began on a day when Riffle woke up not feeling well. As a result, he decided that he was not going to do anything on that day. When the loud speaker called for gunner instructors to report to the planes, he failed to do so. Later that day Riffle heard that the plane that would have carried him had crashed. Despite the grief felt for his fallen airmen, Riffle also felt relieved and blessed.

In February of 1945, Riffle and the other members of the bomb crew were sent to Bautista, Cuba, to teach and practice over-water flying and navigation. On one occasion, after performing their day's routine work, they headed back to the airstrip; as they approached the runway, the landing gear failed to operate. The bomb bay contained a crank for the landing gear. "We cranked and cranked repeatedly until finally the electrical problem with the gear somehow miraculously fixed itself. As this occurred, everybody stood ready with their parachutes. Being the instructor, I had to be the last person out of the back of the plane, because if anyone wouldn't jump, I would have to push them out."

One of Riffle's biggest regrets is he never had the chance to make a jump out of a plane. "If I had a chance to go make a jump tomorrow, I would go, even though it would probably scare me to death," he laughs.

Despite never getting the opportunity to jump, Riffle was required to keep a parachute with him during his flight missions. Every ninety days he sent it to be repacked, and he kept getting encouraged to get rid of it. Riffle resisted, though, because it was lightweight, and he just really liked it. Later on, however, he and some of his friends were surprised to discover that the parachute was defective. Needless to say, Riffle at the time was grateful that he never needed to make a jump!

"If I could go back and have the opportunity to rejoin the Air Force, I wouldn't hesitate one minute before saying yes. It was the best experience in my life, and anybody that got to encounter being a gunner in a plane probably thinks the same," Riffle vows.

Despite the fact that Riffle feels remorse toward those that he trained that never returned from the Pacific, many crewmembers on those B29s did make it home safely, and they can partially thank instructors like Bill Riffle for it. Now in his late eighties, Riffle is widowed and lives in New Haven, West Virginia, where he enjoys his children and grandchildren. And although he seems very happy and satisfied today, it seems evident that he wouldn't mind going back to 1944 all over again.

About the Author. Sam German was raised in West Columbia, West Virginia, by his mother and grandparents. He likes to golf, so he is a member of the varsity golf team at Wahama High School. When not golfing, he enjoys hunting, fishing, and bowling. Besides attending Wahama, he also goes to the Mason County Career Center to learn to be a machinist or a carpenter.

Wahama student-author Sam German poses with World War II veteran and Leon, West Virginia, native Bill Riffle.

Ralph Roush

United States Army
Vietnam War

By Kaula Young

Ralph Roush, many would say, has led a very typical life for someone from Mason County who grew up in the sixties. Raised in New Haven with his three brothers and two sisters, he enjoyed a middle-class childhood. As a teenager, he graduated from Wahama High School and later found work in the local power plants. However, in early adulthood his life's course ran into a major roadblock—one called Vietnam.

In 1965 at age nineteen, Roush received his draft notification. Had he been given a choice, Roush says his would have been obvious: "They would have had to drag me off the hill for me to go." With no other real options, however, he did the same thing as thousands of other young men—he accepted it and served his country. He was selected into the U.S. Army.

Roush's reaction to the news that he was being sent to Vietnam was probably very typical. "I was very scared," he says. When asked how his family took the news, he replied, "My mom took it pretty well." However, it wasn't like Roush's mother was unaccustomed to this kind of news, for both of his older brothers served in World War II.

Once in Vietnam, Roush reported to Camron Bay in 1966. "There really wasn't much there except a big sand dune." When asked what other first impressions he had of the country, he replied, "I don't really remember that much about it. We got off the boat and started in." Roush explains that for about the first week, he and the others that arrived with him did not see much; instead, they grew used to their immediate surroundings and new living conditions. "It was not a fun experience at all."

Roush stayed in Camron Bay for a short time before transferring to a more northern location for about seven months. "We were never really in one particular place for very long though," he states.

Among the many memories of his duties includes the busy schedule that he maintained, citing sixteen-hour days, seven days a week. Roush served in a transportation outfit. "It was just like a job. We drove trucks, often hauling ammunition or fuel. Sometimes you were on the road for twenty-four hours. You'd finally get back to your base camp, be asleep for three or four hours, and someone would come and wake you up for guard duty." Guard duty often lasted for sixteen hours, which was a cycle of two hours on, followed by two hours off. "You were a soldier first. You pulled guard duty. You did everything a soldier would do."

One of the toughest times Roush experienced in Vietnam was driving in convoys. "The North Vietnamese always blew the middle of the convoys up to separate them, and then they attacked some of the trucks in the back." On one occasion, the truck he drove was hit, causing him to veer into the weeds. The next thing he knew, he and the other men were under attack. "I couldn't find my weapon; it probably had flown out of the truck," states Roush. The enemy advance lasted only a couple of minutes, and Roush luckily survived after the assault was met with ample resistance. "We got out of it because of air power. Those planes came in and dropped napalm on those guys attacking us."

When not transporting supplies as a truck driver, Roush took part in what he called "search and destroy" missions. "That was not a pleasant experience," he confessed. Oftentimes, he and the other men in his unit would be out for up to twenty days at a time. "You'd be tired, hungry, and cold. At camp, we had cots inside our tents, but we really didn't have much opportunity to use them. We were always on the road or someplace else."

However, the worst part of Roush's war experience came when they left Camron Bay. "It never seemed to stop raining. It constantly rained and rained and rained. You just stayed wet." This also made it difficult to keep his clothing dry, especially socks, and it was important for soldiers to have dry feet. "Your clothes would rot right off of you," he remembers.

Along the lines of personal hygiene, Roush comments that it unfortunately was almost nonexistent. "I had the opportunity to brush my teeth maybe ten times during the whole year I was there. The only exception was when I was on R and R in Japan. Then I think I brushed them about twelve times a day just because it felt so good. Getting a chance to shave or take a bath was minimal, and that was one of the really hard parts about being there."

Because of the bland food, eating in Vietnam was viewed mainly as a necessity only. Roush and thousands of other soldiers relied on C-rations, which he recalls were simply not very tasty.

Roush also mentions that his youthful age played a role in his many apprehensions. "I was just nineteen when I was over there, and I didn't know what to expect from day to day. Being afraid was also very tough." Roush admits that the war was nothing like he thought it would be. He remembers how little kids would often walk up with live grenades, killing the kids and everyone around them. "I didn't expect it to be like that," he says. He explains that he expected to be attacked at night and shot at in the daytime, but the little kids and women who were used and manipulated by the enemy came as a huge surprise.

"If you really had to sum up everything about the Vietnam War," says Roush, "it would be that it was a political war, although I didn't realize that until I got over there. When I got home I found out it was just for nothing. We really didn't have a reason to go over there. I felt like I was doing something while I was over there. It was a bad place to be, but if I had it to do over again, I'd do the same thing. It was a place where you felt alive, like you were doing something." Later, however, Roush realized that the dead bodies he had seen were for a reason. "The first few that I saw were just bodies. After that, though, it became tougher to live with." After awhile, dreams of his experiences began during the nights. "You saw God-awful things over there," he said.

Finally, one day while in a convoy, Roush received the news he had been longing to hear. "They came and got me, and then after they took me back to the base, I was put on a helicopter. Seventy-two hours later, I was home."

Altogether, Roush spent eleven months and twenty-six days in Vietnam, and luckily, he incurred no major injuries. He characterized life back home as "kind of crazy" for a while. The major problem was that after coming back, there was really no one around to talk to about his experience. "The soldiers that came home by ship had a couple of weeks to talk to each other. I didn't have the opportunity for that sharing of feelings about the dreams and things of that nature." Another problem was that many American citizens failed to recognize Vietnam veterans like Roush in a positive way. "They spit at us and threw stuff at us. Many called us dope-smoking baby killers." Roush believes that as combat veterans, he and his fellow soldiers should have been welcomed back without the negative responses. "It really broke my heart in a way."

As a child, Roush had contracted polio, and although it did little to hamper his physical abilities while in Vietnam, all the walking and physical stress he endured in Southeast Asia did lead to several problems years afterward. "Being constantly cold and wet really took a toll on my legs," he says.

Despite the recurring dreams and bad memories that linger from an experience that Roush would often just soon forget, he says that he is "tickled to death" to have served his country. Upon his return, he took a job with the power company and stayed there until his retirement in October of 2008. Today, Roush remains active in the American Legion and enjoys his life with his wife, Sheila, three children, and eight grandchildren.

Front left: student-author Taylor Hysell, Vietnam War veteran Ralph Roush, and student-author Kaula Young.

Jeff Russell

United States Army National Guard
Operation Iraqi Freedom

By Michael Fisher

The American military experience has truly proven fruitful for Jeff Russell, for early in his adult life, the Mason resident decided to make a career out of the National Guard. This vocation, however, can have its pratfalls, and Russell knows all about them. Without a doubt the most serious, not to mention life-threatening, event occurred in December of 2003 when he and other members of the 1st Battalion 150th Armor were deployed to Iraq for 15 months. Russell, though, views his time spent in the Middle East with a positive slant that has made him appreciate his life in the United States.

Born on August 10, 1958, to Dorothy Jean Russell and his late father who he never knew, Jeff Russell was raised in a family with a lot of affiliation in the military. This prompted Russell at the age of seventeen to enlist in the Army National Guard. He also thought it would be the most patriotic thing to do. The training he endured was one of the most challenging experiences of his young life. "When you enter the military, you are under what's called a structured environment. Everything is planned for you: what time you're going to get up, what time you eat chow, what time you do PT, what time you get to shower, what time you go to training, what time you eat lunch, more training, when you eat dinner, and how much time you have before lights are out, and they even tell you when you're going to sleep." It was what Russell calls a culture change. He always had someone telling him what to do, where to go, and how to do it. They drilled it into Russell over and over again to the point that where anything that happened to him became second nature with a reaction. Russell said that when he trained, he learned that he had to have that second nature instinct to be able to be in the military.

Although the Guard taught him the trade of a maintenance technician, Russell also trained in anything that he was told. In December 2003, he and his unit were deployed to Iraq. Knowing what kind of environment to expect, he wasn't surprised to be in the desert settings of the Middle East. He and his unit were assigned to patrol and defend a certain sector, which just happened to be one of the biggest there, roughly 350 square miles. This didn't affect Russell's attitude at all. "If anything, it was just another culture change," he said.

Russell's unit arrived in Iraq just after the war ended, so they more or less were in clean-up mode. While overseas, Russell found himself in many interesting locations. "I was in several different parts of Iraq. I was in Baghdad, I was in Balad, and I was on the Iranian border for a while. But we just moved as the mission changed." Russell states that he was never really nervous or scared to be there, and after a while, he didn't even turn his head when he heard a loud boom.

Although we often hear negative feedback from the news media about the Iraqi citizens, Russell says most of the people saw the American soldiers as the heroes, not the enemies. The enemies, however, were the people trying to keep the country dictatorial. The people as a whole appreciated what the troops did for them and showed them gratitude. In fact, Russell's unit took an interpreter with them everywhere that they went so that they could contact the people and interact with them directly in order to insure positive public relations. Russell said, "We have helped them come from being an oppressed, controlled people under a cruel dictatorship to a free nation with a new government and new freedoms. To see those people have the rights that Americans have had for two hundred and thirty-three years is one of the best memories I have."

Russell and the other members of his unit were forced to adapt to new living conditions very abruptly while in Iraq. There were no luxuries, such as television or radio, for entertainment. However, they were provided with a small computer room with six computers, and they each received about ten to fifteen minutes of time every day to email their friends and family back home. Although entertainment was scarce, Russell recalls a time coming back from a mission that he and his unit watched a USO show. Other means of enjoyment came from playing practical jokes on his buddies. "Yeah, you had your usual practical jokes you played on your buddies: sewing up their sleeping bags, hiding their shaving kits, and stuff like that," he laughed. In addition to these humorous events, Russell recalls an unfortunate mishap that made him laugh. One day, he and a few of his buddies were sitting on the back step of a stoop when they heard a boom. They looked out and saw a rocket coming right toward the compound, and it hit one of their eighty-eight tanker troopers about eighty yards from where they sat. The funny part to Russell was that it blew the track off of it, and they had just finished putting that brand new track on it not even an hour beforehand. "There you sit, and you watch some clown fire a rocket, and you watch it hit that track and blow it off after all of that work." Even though several light moments like this existed, most of his memories were of a more serious magnitude.

The hardest part of Russell's military experience was leaving his family behind. As hard as it was for him to do this, he and his wife, son, and daughter knew that this was part of the job. They understood the risks that he was taking when he left for service. This wasn't all bad for Russell, however. He received a Bronze Star, the Iraqi Campaign Ribbon, and a few other overseas ribbons for his service to the United States. Today he is a member of the Veterans of Foreign Wars and the American Legion. Russell continues to work for the West Virginia National Guard at the Eleanor Maintenance Facility in Eleanor, West Virginia. Being in the military has made him look at his life and appreciate its value. He concluded by saying, "If I had the chance, I'd go back and do it again."

About the Author: Michael Fisher, 16, is lifelong resident of Mason County and currently resides in the town of Mason, West Virginia. He is a senior at Wahama High School and an active member of the Fairview Bible Church Youth Group. In his spare time, Michael likes to hang out with his friends and play guitar. When he turns seventeen, he plans on enlisting in the Army National Guard. Although he doesn't know which school he will attend after high school, Michael plans on getting a degree in teaching. This future Wahama graduate hopes to make something good out of his life.

Operation Iraqi Freedom veteran Jeff Russell answers questions by student-author Michael Fisher.

Carl Swisher

United States Army
Vietnam War

By Zach Whitlatch

Carl Swisher, his face flushed red, sits hesitantly in the interview room. As he speaks, he often looks down for long periods at the empty table on which his elbow leans. He has anxiously waited for this chance to speak about his combat experiences for some time, yet nervous trepidation persists. "This will be on my mind again now for two or three days," says Swisher of his combat experiences as a young man. His story of remembrance is very familiar to that of thousands of Vietnam veterans.

As a teenager Swisher desperately wanted to enlist and serve his country. However, one major problem existed—he wasn't old enough. Eager to join up and too impatient to wait until his eighteenth birthday, he simply lied about his age. When he admits this today, Swisher speaks it with some apprehension as well as a little shame, but this showed his willingness to serve his country at the time. "At eighteen you either enlisted in the service or signed up for the draft. I enlisted in the Army," states Swisher.

Upon his enlistment, Swisher really didn't know that he would be sent to Vietnam, although it was a pretty safe assumption at that time. His first stop, however, was Fort Knox, Kentucky, for basic training. From there, the Army dispatched him to Fort Gordon, Georgia, for a type of more specialized training. From Georgia it was on to Hawaii, where he received his toughest training to date, for here the Army taught him how to survive during guerilla warfare. In fact, this was so intense that it lasted for nine months. Afterward, the Army felt Swisher was finally ready to perform the task in which he had trained. His next stop would be Vietnam in December 1965. Swisher felt well prepared to enter the war.

When first arriving in Vietnam, Swisher and the other new arrivals were not immediately thrown into action. "We went up on what they called 'Gun Hill' and there set up what we called a community. About the first three weeks were for setting camps up, such as tents and shelters. We dug shelters for artillery."

One recollection Swisher remembers most about his first weeks in Vietnam was the revelation of having so much live ammunition, along with the responsibility of securing many areas. His first major job in the war-torn country consisted of serving in a convoy with around one hundred and twenty other men. These convoys proved very important to the war effort in Vietnam. Their major role was to transport supplies to various posts. Swisher knows this because he led the particular convoy in which he was a member. The principal components of these convoys were six "106" jeeps with fifty-caliber M-60's mounted on them, two three-quarter ton trucks with M-50 machine guns, and a couple of other trucks with purposes for carrying supplies as well as additional items.

As part of these convoys, Swisher and his fellow soldiers received enemy fire on two occasions, but nothing really serious. Swisher explains, "We ran on one of the main highways, and there was little action. Sometimes there would just be some sniper fire."

After about three months of convoys, Swisher's responsibilities changed. He now found himself on helicopter missions looking for enemy stations located in the country's vast mountains. "I didn't like that," he states. "After we secured these areas, we set up ambushes along the trails. It was very dangerous in the helicopters, and we lost a lot of men." In fact, Swisher lost many friends in combat.

On October 25, 1966, Swisher's life changed dramatically during a helicopter assault. Swisher jumped out of his helicopter in the midst of a dangerous mission assisting a battalion on the ground. He recalls having to jump far from the ground because the bamboo was up pretty high. The enemy had many primitive traps set there, making for the perilous jump. As a result of these extreme combat conditions, Swisher sustained a severe injury that shortened his tour. "There was no place for a helicopter to set down in order to rescue me, but there was a pilot that by God's grace was able to somehow get his helicopter down." This enabled Swisher to get out of this very delicate situation. Once well enough to travel, he was transported to a hospital in the Philippines (where he spent his nineteenth birthday) and then on to Japan, where he remained in the hospital until December 10, 1966. "I really wanted to be home for Christmas," says Swisher, and he did make it.

Looking back on his other remembrances of the Vietnam War, Swisher recalls that recognizing the enemy was sometimes difficult. "Vietnam was a differently-fought war altogether. Sometimes before you would go out on a mission, it would be broadcast that it [the mission] was coming to this certain area so all the 'friendlies' could get out. But you couldn't always tell the friendlies from the enemies. Therefore, you treated everybody as an enemy until they proved you wrong." The local people did treat them with the respect they deserved and were very kind. "They welcomed us with open arms and treated us tremendously," remembers Swisher.

Swisher does not recall really having any time for anything other than his missions. He often even found eating a difficult task because of the lack of down time. Eating sometimes took place on the helicopter to or from missions. His longest time without a full meal was forty days, but they usually ate one hot meal once a week. It wasn't unusual for Swisher and his troops to trade something to the friendlies in exchange for a chicken. When free time existed, there wasn't really anything to do. Sometimes, however, a projector would be set up, and the men would have an opportunity to watch a movie. In addition, according to Swisher, "Every now and then they might ship in some actor or singer to entertain the troops." Sometimes when they had free time on their hands, they would go to the nearest town to just get out of the base.

When asked if people treated him differently when he returned home from Vietnam, Swisher replied, "I believe most people were appreciative, but I think the stigmatism that came with most Vietnam vets from the news media was the connotation of them being child killers and other different scenarios. So you had many mixed emotions. I had emotions of I think I served my country very well, but overall there were many emotional roller coasters on everyone's part." When asked about the lasting personal effects of the Vietnam War on his life, Swisher replied, "Any moments from war will result in effects."

Once home and discharged from the military, most things returned to normal for Swisher—that is, except for the flashbacks of the negative encounters he experienced. Despite the bad memories, flashbacks, and occasional nightmares, Swisher vows that he would not take anything back and would do it all again for his country.

Today Carl Swisher enjoys his life with his family. Several years after his tour in Vietnam, he felt called to enter the ministry, and today he pastors the First Church of God in Point Pleasant, West Virginia. In addition, he loves fishing and played softball and ran for exercise in his younger days. Swisher, like so many of the men and women who served our country during wartime, displays the utmost humility in regards to his contributions in Vietnam. But just like all those others who risked their lives for us all, he is truly a hero.

About the Author. Zachary Whitlatch lives in Hartford, West Virginia, with his mom. He loves playing basketball and shooting and practicing as much as he can. When he is not doing this, he likes to hang out with his girlfriend and with his friends. After high school he plans to attend a small college where he can play basketball and get a scholarship.

In October 1966, Carl Swisher sustained a severe injury during a helicopter assault in Vietnam.

Billy Van Meter

United States Army
World War II

By Deidra Peters

On October 3, 1942, Billy Van Meter's life changed forever. The United States had been involved in World War II for less than a year, and the military drafted thousands of young men to participate on two battle fronts. For Van Meter, being drafted took an extreme emotional toll, for he left behind a pregnant wife. However, despite the hardship of saying goodbye to loved ones, Van Meter did his duty and prospered in his role in the European Theater of Operations.

Upon being drafted into the Army at age twenty-one, Van Meter was inducted in Huntington, West Virginia. From there, he left for Atlantic City, New Jersey, and Fort Myers, Florida, for training. His final stop before going overseas was a site in Minnesota. "It was forty degrees below zero," he chuckled. Once sent to Europe, the Army assigned him to the 8th Air Force stationed at Bury St. Edmunds, England, a few miles inland from the English Channel. Traveling to England, Van Meter recalls that he wasn't really scared or apprehensive. "I was wondering what in the world was in store for us." He spent his first two years of service there.

Van Meter's main duty in the Air Force was to drive what he called a gasoline train. He pulled two four-thousand gallon tankers full of octane fuel to be put into planes. "I had to keep one tank empty all the time," he says, "so when a plane crashed I could have somewhere to siphon the gas back out. That way it wouldn't be lost." Van Meter admits that this could sometimes be a dangerous job because "the engines would be smoking and I'd be up on a wing sucking that gas out." Van Meter also oversaw a smaller truck with lower-octane fuel for the smaller planes.

While stationed in England, Van Meter described his living conditions as very comfortable. "I had no complaints," he says. However, sometimes dangerous predicaments arose. He recalls one particular night when things were a little frightening during an air raid warning. "When we got an air raid warning, we'd go out and get in a ditch. About the time we got to the door, this bomb landed next to us. We turned around and ran right back to the barracks." Despite that scary predicament, Van Meter said that rarely did the air base on which he was stationed ever get raided. "Before I got there though, it had been attacked regularly, and you could see evidence of it all around," he said.

Van Meter recalls being in England during the D-Day invasion. "On that day you could look up in the sky, and it was just black. Every plane was airborne. It was like this for about three days." Van Meter says that he and the other men knew that the Normandy invasion was going to happen and looked forward to it. They were just not aware of the exact day. "A lot of preparation went into that," he says.

While in Great Britain, Van Meter says that the American servicemen were treated very nicely by the English people. "They treated us great. I have no complaints." He recalls one couple who graciously offered to give him rides or let him stay over if he ever missed his truck going to or from town. In fact, after the war, Van Meter continued to correspond with them briefly. "I still have letters and a picture of them at home. Of course, we were over there to save those people." He remembers that in spite of the dire situation that the English citizens were in, they still managed to be resilient and confident. "They did a good job of holding off the Nazis for as long as they did."

One of the assets of being a truck driver was that Van Meter was able to travel around the English countryside. However, he recalls the roads being difficult to navigate. He says, "If you didn't know where you were going, you were probably lost to begin with. I've followed telephone lines all day long trying to find the base."

During one of his experiences, Van Meter led a convoy to Belgium in 1944. They crossed the English Channel by ship into France, where they spent seven days and nights camped along the mouth of the Seine River. This was due to a battle taking place in their planned direct line of travel. "We each had only one blanket, and we nearly froze to death. I tried to get the captain to allow us to build a fire, but he refused to permit it. He finally let us start one in a barrel on the ship."

Upon their arrival in Belgium, Van Meter and his men began receiving enemy fire from a hospital. "We went into the hospital and got about two truckloads and a busload of German soldiers out of there. They weren't even supposed to have been in that hospital. They had been hiding in there." Even though he wasn't hit by enemy fire during this episode, he sustained a broken foot, although he isn't to this day exactly sure how it happened. This turned out to be the only time that Van Meter was subjected to enemy fire.

The most difficult part of Van Meter's war experience wasn't fear or physical duress; instead, it was being away from wife Dorothy. In fact, as he prepared to go overseas, the couple was expecting their first child. While Van Meter traveled to Little Falls, Minnesota, Dorothy gave birth to their son Donnie. "I was on my way to Minnesota, and I got the call that I had a baby boy." To try to ease matters, Van Meter became close with many of the men with which he served. He remembers that one time while training in New Jersey, he arrived to his barracks late at night to find a soldier sleeping in his bunk. "He was a little inebriated, and we argued until he finally got up and out of my bunk. He and I ended up going to England together and becoming the best of friends. The men over there became my family for the time that I was there. You'd do just about anything for them, and they'd do the same for you."

When Van Meter entered the Army a second time, he volunteered as a rifleman for an infantry group that served as replacements. "In case they needed to fill in an empty spot, someone would be there," commented Van Meter on the role of these replacement groups. In order to join the infantry, he had to go back for more training. "During infantry training I was a squad leader," he said. Van Meter, however, did not see any combat. "I tried," he said, "but I couldn't get in."

Van Meter related a very interesting story in regard to his joining the infantry: "My best friend got killed. I just thought I'd go over there and help end it real quickly," he says, tearfully. "Unfortunately, I didn't get to do anything that I'd hope for, because they just didn't need me, I guess." Van Meter continued by saying that in October 2007, he and some family members traveled to Washington, D.C., to visit the World War II Memorial, where he located the name "Chester Cartwright"—his best friend killed in action. It was quite a moving experience for Van Meter and brought back bittersweet memories.

On October 10, 1945, three years and one week to the day that he was drafted, Van Meter received his honorable discharge from the Army. "I was on my way home when the war ended," he says. "I liked serving my country in the military. I really wouldn't change anything." Nowadays, although he says he really can't do much anymore due to the consequences of age, Van Meter and Dorothy travel to Florida every year to spend the winter months. When not in Florida, the couple resides at their home in Clifton, West Virginia.

Billy Van Meter, here with his wife Dorothy, was stationed in England for the majority of his time in World War II.

Marcellus Waid

United States Navy
World War II and Korean War

By Lindsey Deem

As a teenager during the World War II era, many young men were forced to make some difficult choices, such as whether or not to graduate from high school. Most knew that some type of military service awaited, and it was often just a matter of enlisting or waiting for selection via the draft. These tough decisions, however, were easy for a then-eighteen-year-old resident of Roanoke, Virginia, named Marcellus Waid, who already had two older brothers serving in the U.S. Navy in World War II.

Born on June 6, 1926, Waid's young life got off to a terrible start with the passing of his mother, Ora, when he was just nine. This left his father, Charles Waid, a widower in charge of raising young Marcellus and his brothers by himself. Many difficulties emerged as a result, mainly because Charles worked most of the time in order to make a humble and meager living for him and his sons. Marcellus' Aunt Una, however, played a huge role in raising him, and he gives her much credit for taking care of him.

As his high school graduation approached, Waid realized that college would not be an option due to the huge costs. Knowing that his two brothers were already in the Navy and having heard their stories, he decided to continue the line of Waid brothers taking to the seas and enlisted. One barrier, however, still existed: finishing school.

On his eighteenth birthday on June 6, 1944, Waid received two "presents." One was his high school diploma. He graduated at ten in the morning. The other present was a trip out of town. At approximately four o'clock Waid left for the Navy. Coincidentally, this day was also "D-Day." He jokes, "That's the reason why Hitler gave up, because they sent me in." Needless to say, he was ready to get his adult life started after high school. In fact, he got it started by becoming involved in the largest conflict that this country has ever seen—World War II.

Waid served in the Navy during the war's final months aboard a salvage tug, which rescued ships in distress or in danger of sinking. They towed ships, barges, and platforms; they also performed various kinds of utility work. "Ships would often lose their screw or their rudder," says Waid, "and we would have to go out and get them." Waid recalls one humorous moment when he threw a heaving line, a rope used to tie onto other ships, over the rail to get it wet, which was a common practice. "I made the mistake of throwing it aside right when the captain put the ship in reverse. The line got tangled up in the rudder, and I got called out for that. I felt pretty low for a while after that, especially since I think I was the first on our crew that had ever done it."

Waid's job on board the ship was a signalman, which was a communication specialist aboard naval vessels. "I had to learn Morse code and became pretty good at it. I prepared headings and addresses for outgoing messages, I processed messages, and I encoded and decoded them." In addition, Waid performed duties consisting of carrying out look-out and visual recognition signals.

Waid remembers that his particular job as a signalman required working some strange schedules. For instance, he usually worked four hours and then would have eight off. "I often worked from midnight to four in the morning, and afterwards all I wanted to do was sleep," he laughs.

Waid admits that since he was still quite young, he often got homesick. Receiving mail helped a little. Being on a ship in the middle of the sea, however, often made it difficult to receive letters from home. "A lot of it got to us kind of late, but it really wasn't that bad." Waid wrote mainly to family. "I actually got quite a lot of mail." News didn't travel well either onto the ship. "We usually received news of events sometime afterwards," he says. When asked what their longest amount of time was out to sea, Waid stated, "I can't really remember." He explained that often, time aboard the ship seemed to fly by, but other times it crept along, thus making it difficult to keep track of time. "They really kept us busy," he remembers.

One advantage, however, of being on a ship was that Waid and the others aboard always got hot food to eat, as opposed to those in other military branches. His biggest complaint was the coffee. "They served us hot coffee for breakfast but then they gave us the leftover coffee the rest of the day, and it was always cold."

When the ship docked, Waid and his fellow sailors were given liberty, or shore leave, for short periods of time, usually twelve hours. Many times during liberty, he and his friends went to movie theaters, played cards, or visited the nearest towns. On many of these excursions, Waid's best friend on board the ship, Jack Parkerson, accompanied him.

Some of the ports in which Waid stopped included many along the Mediterranean and the Sea of Japan. He kept a detailed log of everywhere he went, calculating that during his naval tenure he sailed over a million miles. Another memorable destination was across the North Pole near Barrow, Alaska. "We had to take an ice breaker, which was a ship that goes ahead of another ship, to break the ice." His most special site, though, was the Rock of Gibraltar, which he vividly recalls being covered with monkeys.

Waid remembers his ship being docked in Norfolk, Virginia, when the war ended. Although he doesn't necessarily recall a lot of wild celebrations, he did say, "We were definitely happy to be getting out [of the War]. I remember hearing the captain say that we could have anything aboard the ship to eat or drink."

Waid's discharge finally came in 1946; however, he was still considered to be on reserve duty, and four years later, he found himself being activated once again. The Korean conflict had begun, and many men in addition to Waid were being called back. In fact, both of his brothers also were recalled. It had been just five years since the Japanese and German surrenders, and now once again our nation faced another war. Waid recalls that even though there was a great amount of support from the American people, some felt bitterness to be back in wartime.

For this war, Waid served on a different kind of ship—a tanker. It delivered gasoline and oil. Waid says his biggest fear regarding this type of ship was the large amount of fuel that it often carried. He and several of his shipmates worried on many occasions about the threat of a bomb striking them while holding such a cargo. Despite the change of ships, his job of signalman remained the same, and he earned the rank of Third-class Petty Officer for performing it well. After serving two years in the Korean War, Waid was discharged again, this time for good. "The day I finally got out is a day that I'll always remember. I felt blessed to be alive and thankful to see my family and friends once again."

Upon returning home, Waid attained a job working for the power company, which soon after brought him to Mason County, where he met his wife. He stayed at a boarding house just up the street from where she lived, and they worked at the same plant. They soon began dating and married six weeks later. "You could call it love at first sight," chuckled Waid. They later added two children to the family—Susan, the oldest, followed by Mark.

Throughout his war experience, Marcellus Waid, like all veterans, made a difference. He felt obligated to join because of his unfortunate childhood and because his two brothers were already in the Navy. What he did not know at the time was that his hard work and bravery contributed to the freedom of this country. Not only did he play a big role for two years in World War II, but he served in the Korean War as well. Today at the age of eighty-three, he has much in which to be proud.

About the Author. Lindsey Danielle Deem and her family currently reside in Mason, West Virginia. She is a senior at Wahama High School. Her mother, aunts, and uncle are the most important people in her life. She enjoys playing softball and other sports. After high school, she plans on attending college and pursuing her career in the medical field.

Eager to join the military, Marcellus Waid left for the Navy on the same day as his high school graduation.

Leon Yoder

United States Army
Korean War Veteran

By Ethan McGrew

Leon Yoder feels privileged to have gained the opportunity to serve in the United States Army during the Korean War. Ironically, the Point Pleasant resident never stepped foot on Korean soil. This, however, was not uncommon, for thousands of wartime veterans were never deployed to war zones; instead, they protected our country and its interests in other ways. In fact, in the early 1950s the Army stationed Yoder in Germany, which was intriguing for two reasons: Germany's reconstruction after World War II and its strategic position as an instrumental pawn during the early years of the Cold War.

Yoder's military story began in 1952. The country, still recovering from the mass casualties and huge expenses of World War II, suddenly found itself in another conflict—the Korean War. Yoder remembers the attitudes shared by most Americans at that time: "Our country wasn't really prepared for another war, but as soldiers, we were very well accepted. The country seemed to support our efforts, unlike what happened several years later in Vietnam."

The Army selected Yoder through the draft. "At this time, you were drafted for two years of active duty and six years of reserves," says Yoder. "After eight years, you received your discharge." Yoder recalls that every male registered for the draft at the age of eighteen, much like today. Upon being drafted, a person would get called up to report to a particular destination for a physical to determine if the draftee was physically able to join the military. After that, young men waited for their turns to come, based upon the Army's needs and the person's name. "The group that I took my physical with was almost all gone and drafted before me because of my last name of Yoder. They usually selected alphabetically."

Yoder performed basic training in Fort Breckenridge, Kentucky, which was also where the 101st Airborne Unit was stationed for training purposes only. While there, Yoder trained in light infantry for sixteen weeks. "I actually enjoyed the first half of basic training," smiled Yoder. "I started the day after

Labor Day in 1952. It was warm and dry that year, and I kept thinking, 'This isn't bad.'" However, things changed dramatically around the week of Thanksgiving when Yoder and his fellow soldiers went out into the field. They awoke one morning to find about two inches of snow on the ground. It later turned to rain. "At that time we were out in the bunkers, and it was wet and muddy and cold," he recalls. Yoder remembers thinking at the time: "How do I get out of this?"

Not long afterward, Yoder's luck changed. The Army assigned him and two others to six additional weeks of schooling at Fort Benjamin Harrison in Indiana. This proved to be a huge turning point in Yoder's military commitment, for he would now be given the opportunity for a more specialized job. It was opportunities such as this that may have possibly kept Yoder from an assignment to Korea.

"My battalion was made up of four companies," states Yoder. "A-Company was sent to the Far East, which meant Korea, and both B- and D-Companies went there as well. C-Company, which is what I was in, was for the most part sent to England; but because of my additional training, I was sent to Germany."

During most of his tenure in the Army, Yoder was stationed in Germany as part of the occupation forces that stabilized that country after World War II. Yoder was assigned to a machine records unit, which used what nowadays would seem like very primitive computers. These machines implemented punch cards to keep track of personnel and equipment.

A typical day for Yoder consisted of waking up around six o'clock, participating in a short period of calisthenics, and eating breakfast. Following the morning meal, Yoder headed to his office to perform his duties. His office routine was similar to that of most civilians: clock in by eight, break an hour for lunch, and leave at five. After a busy day at the office, Yoder was free to do what he wanted. "You had to get a pass to go to town, but pretty much your time was your own after you did your duties."

Yoder remembers that the base where he was stationed had many German civilians on it. They worked and were paid by the American soldiers to do all the kitchen duties and the cleaning. "Then in the PX, they had German barbers and some with other occupations, so there were a lot of Germans that worked on the base."

Yoder arrived in Germany only seven years after the United States and its Allies defeated the Germans in World War II. Admitting that it was a little strange to be in a country that had just been defeated largely in part by American forces, he recalls that many of the German people still acted bitter; however, most were very cordial and helpful. "It was kind of a mixed thing. Some of them hated your guts, but then there were some nice German people.

They were making money off of us though, like in their restaurants—but for the most part, they were nice." Yoder admits, however, that since most of his fellow soldiers could not speak the native language, the Germans probably said some bad things about their American "guests."

Even with lots of time on their hands during the evenings, Yoder says that there really wasn't much for him and his friends to do in their spare time. He did recall, though, that the Army provided a bus that took the men around to various spots. One of Yoder's most vivid memories was when he and two of his buddies took a four-day leave to England. In addition, Yoder recalls taking a train to Zurich, Switzerland, which he stated as being beautiful. Also, the Army base sponsored a bingo night, where prizes were awarded.

Yoder states that even though it had been less than a decade since World War II, he saw no signs of what was formerly the Nazi regime. "We were limited to what we saw. You have to remember that at this time, Germany was split up into the East and West. The United States occupied West Germany, while Russia controlled East Germany. The Russians and Americans shared control of the city of Berlin." Yoder remembers that at times activity outside of the base was limited because of both German and Russian threats. "May Day was the big holiday for the Russians," according to Yoder, "so we would be restricted as to what we could do both on and off the base on May 1st."

Germany in 1952 still showed the destruction left behind by Allied forces as they marched through the country toward the end of World War II. "When we were on the train that took us to our base, we traveled through several towns that were completely destroyed, but they were rebuilding just about everywhere." He recalls one of the passengers on the train who had been to Germany a few years before seeing a town and saying, "The last time I came through here, there wasn't a building standing."

With Yoder's time in Germany finally complete, he proceeded to travel back home. He remembers the people of his native country treating him very nicely when he reached the United States. "People recognized that you had been in the military and appreciated you." Overall, Yoder thoroughly enjoyed his time in the military. "It was a great experience. I was offered an extra stripe if I re-upped, but I decided it was time for me to go back home." In addition, he had a civilian job waiting on him.

Nearly sixty years ago, Leon Yoder was drafted like many other young American men of his time. Although he considers himself very fortunate that he didn't have to serve in Korea, he says he would have proudly fought if required. In fact, many soldiers of Yoder's day were stationed in various places other than Korea, and they played an integral role in protecting our nation. Today, Yoder is retired and enjoys spending time with his wife, Isabelle, his

children, and his grandchildren. He enjoys church, traveling, and going out
to eat with Isabelle.

About the Author: Ethan McGrew is a resident of Mason, West Virginia,
and a senior at Wahama High School, where he enjoys playing football and
baseball for the White Falcons. He also enjoys hunting, fishing, and hanging
with his friends in his spare time when he isn't at school.

During the Korean War, the Army stationed Leon Yoder in Germany.